Ramesses the Great
His Life and World

Presented by the City of Memphis, Tennessee
and the Egyptian Antiquities Organization
in cooperation with
Memphis Brooks Museum of Art
and
the Institute of Egyptian Art and Archaeology,
Memphis State University

Rita E. Freed

Ramesses the Great

This exhibition is supported by an indemnity from the Federal Council on the Arts and Humanities.

Library of Congress Cataloging-in-Publication Data
Freed, Rita E.
  Ramesses the Great.

  Bibliography: p.
  Includes index.
  1. Egypt--Antiquities--Exhibitions. 2. Ramses II,
King of Egypt.   3. Egypt--Civilization--To 332 B.C.
I. Memphis (Tenn.) II. Title.
DT59.M45F73 1987   932.014'0924 (B)   87-6645
ISBN 0-918518-57-1
ISBN 0-918518-56-3 (pbk.)

Project Coordinator: Nancy E. Bogatin
Graphic Design: Polly Sexton
Editor: Liz Conway
Consulting Editor: Carol Lynn Yellin
Contributing Editor: Valerie Moore
Technical Editors: Anna Kay Walker, Lynn Gipson
Index Compilation: Catherine C. Swearingen
Color Separations and Printing: Lithograph Printing Company
Typography: Marcol Graphics of Memphis

Contents

Beo Carlson

The great civilization of Egypt has for centuries awed and inspired travelers, writers, historians and all people who have been fortunate enough to come in contact with it.

With its naming by the founding fathers, our city, Memphis on the Mississippi, established for itself a unique tie to ancient Memphis, its namesake, and to the people of Egypt.

In modern times, the "new" Memphis has cultivated meaningful relations with Egypt. The signing of a Friendship Agreement with the Governate of Giza and the development of close ties with Egyptian officials both in Washington, D.C. and in Cairo have secured for Memphis a lasting relationship with the people of Egypt.

As a reflection of this closeness between our two peoples, Memphis sought and became the first United States city chosen to host the prestigious Ramesses The Great Exhibition. This generous consideration by the Egyptian Antiquities Organization affords Memphis and the Mid-South region of the United States a rare opportunity to gain a broader understanding of not only Egypt's past, but of the history of mankind.

Of special significance, the project to restore a colossal statue of Ramesses II, which was discovered at ancient Memphis, and to host in Memphis, Tennessee, the

world premiere showing of this great artwork is a reflection of the warm spirit of friendship and the uniqueness of our association with Egypt and the Egyptian people.

To the leadership of the Egyptian Antiquities Organization, especially Dr. Ahmed Kadry, and to His Excellency El Sayad Abdel Raouf El Reedy, Ambassador of Egypt, as well as our corporate sponsors and all others who contributed to the success of this worthwhile endeavor, I wish to express my appreciation for their role in making available this historic event to the people of Memphis and the Mid-South region.

Finally, a debt of gratitude is extended to Helen Scheidt for bringing this worthy project to my attention, to James Broughton who has guided this endeavor to fruition, and to the dedicated and professional staff of the exhibition.

Richard C. Hackett
Mayor of Memphis

A Message from the Chairman of the Egyptian Antiquities Organization

This magnificent exhibition of seventy-three treasures from the time of Pharaoh Ramesses the Great is a landmark event in the history of cultural relations between the American and Egyptian peoples. Many of these priceless objects are from the ancient city of Memphis on the Nile so it is most appropriate that they now be displayed in modern Memphis on the Mississippi. The Egyptian Antiquities Organization is proud to have accepted Mayor Richard Hackett's invitation to display these artifacts in one of America's greatest cities.

Ramesses II was one of Egypt's greatest rulers. He reigned for over sixty-six years and, because of his unprecedented building program, has made Egypt virtually an open air museum. He is known not only for the incomparable temples at Abu Simbel, but also for the colossal statuary throughout the land including magnificent temples at Luxor, Karnak, Abydos, Pi-Ramesses and, of course, Memphis.

The Egyptian Antiquities Organization is particularly proud to join hands with the City of Memphis in restoring the Colossus of Memphis. This 47 ton statue of Ramesses the Great last stood in ancient Memphis. It is appropriate that the modern world premiere take place in our sister city of Memphis, Tennessee. The Colossus will eventually be permanently displayed at the National Museum of Egyptian Civilization that will open in Cairo in 1989.

I wish to express a special personal note of appreciation to Mayor Hackett for making this restoration a reality and not a dream.

Dr. Ahmed Kadry
First Under Secretary of State,
Chairman of the Egyptian Antiquities Organization

A Message from the Ambassador of Egypt

I cannot think of a more enchanting place to stage such an important exhibit of the priceless treasures of Ramesses II, than in Memphis, pearl of the Mississippi, and one of the fountains of American culture.

This important cultural event will, I am confident, present the opportunity to millions of Americans to take a magical journey across the golden folds of Egypt's history.

Nothing is more rewarding for someone whose vocation is to promote Egyptian-American relations, than to see these beautiful artifacts representing Egypt's spirit and conveying a message of friendship to our American friends.

Moreover, it is on occasions like these that one realizes that a universal language does exist after all; one that transcends borders and oceans, to convey a message of friendship, peace and understanding.

El Sayed Abdel Raouf El Reedy
The Ambassador of Egypt
Washington, D.C.

Egyptian Honorary Committee

Under the distinguished patronage
of His Excellency Mr. Hosni Mubarak
President of the Arab Republic of Egypt

His Excellency Dr. Atef Mohamed Naguib Sidki
The Prime Minister of the Arab Republic of Egypt

His Excellency Ahmed Esmat Abdel Meguid
The Minister of Foreign Affairs and
Deputy Prime Minister of the Arab Republic of Egypt

His Excellency Dr. Ahmed Heikal
The Minister of Culture of the Arab Republic of Egypt

His Excellency El Sayed Abdel Raouf El Reedy
Ambassador of the Arab Republic of Egypt
to the United States of America

His Excellency Dr. Ahmed Kadry
The First Under Secretary of State
and Chairman of the Egyptian Antiquities Organization

Professor Dr. Gamal Mokhtar
The former President of the Egyptian Antiquities
Organization and member of its Board of Directors

Mr. Ibrahim El-Nawawy
Director General of Egyptian Museums
of the Egyptian Antiquities Organization

Mr. Mohamed Ahmed Mohsen
Director General of Museum Affairs
of the Egyptian Antiquities Organization

Dr. Mohamed Saleh
Director General of the Egyptian Museum, Cairo

Egyptian Organizing Committee

Mr. Ibrahim El-Nawawy
Director General of Egyptian Museums
of the Egyptian Antiquities Organization

Mr. Mohamed Ahmed Mohsen
Director General of Museum Affairs
of the Egyptian Antiquities Organization

Dr. Mohamed Saleh
Director General of the Egyptian Museum, Cairo

Dr. Abdel-Aziz Sadek
Deputy Director General
Center for Documentation on Ancient Egypt
of the Egyptian Antiquities Organization

Mrs. Saneya Abdel Aal
Deputy Director of the Egyptian Museum, Cairo

Mr. Galal Sharawy
Deputy Director of the Egyptian Museum, Cairo

Memphis Honorary Committee

The Honorable Richard C. Hackett, Chairman
Mayor, City of Memphis

Michael D. Rose, Co-Chairman
Chairman and Chief Executive Officer
Holiday Inns, Inc.-Hotel Group

Mrs. Rudi Scheidt, Co-Chairman

J.R. Hyde, III
President
Malone and Hyde, Inc.

Abdel Moneim Osman
General Manager United States
EgyptAir

George Robert Pidgeon, Jr.
President
Coca-Cola Bottling Company of Memphis

Steven G. Rothmeier
President and Chief Executive Officer
Northwest Airlines, Inc.

Frederick W. Smith
Chairman of the Board
Federal Express Corporation

Ronald A. Terry
Chairman and Chief Executive Officer
First Tennessee

Memphis Organizing Committee

Executive Staff

James E. Broughton, *Executive Director*

Dr. Rita E. Freed, *Curator*

Brady Bartusch, *Staff Attorney*

Nancy Douglass, *Executive Secretary*

Sheryl Bowen, *Special Projects Coordinator*

Glen Campbell, *Technical Planning Coordinator*

Twyla Dixon, *Ticket Administration and Group Sales Coordinator*

J. Richard Gruber, *Artistic and Educational Planning Coordinator*

Joe Holt, *Security Manager*

Jack Kyle, *Communications Coordinator*

Robert Tamboli, *Financial Administration Coordinator*

Artistic and Educational Planning
J. Richard Gruber, *Coordinator*

Exhibition Design
 George Sexton Associates
 Bert Sharpe, *Project Consultant*
 Bill Heidrich, *Project Consultant*
 Marilyn Masler, *Project Consultant*

Orientation Theatre
 Baldridge Studios
 Michael Baldridge, *Producer*
 Gil Herron, *Script Writer*
 Plough Foundation

Education
 Patricia Bladon, *Manager*
 Anna Kay Walker, *Assistant Manager*
 Dr. Carol Crown
 Dr. Edward Bleiberg
 Liz Conway
 Darla Linerode
 Steven McKenzie
 Vanessa Robertson
 Mary Scheuner

Special Projects
Sheryl Bowen, *Coordinator*

Gift Shop
 Lotus and Papyrus International, Inc.
 Rifaat Hassan, *Manager*
 Nihal Mazloum, *Assistant Manager*
 Mark Broughton, *Assistant Manager*

Restaurant
 Midland Food Services, Inc.
 Betty Whitehead, *Manager*

Recorded Tour Guide
 Acoustiguide, Inc.
 Barbara Tomcich, *Manager*
 Trish Langlois, *Assistant Manager*
 Toni Bryan, *Script Writer*

Volunteer Administration
 Junior League of Memphis
 Jane Faquin, *Coordinator*
 Julie Raines, *Coordinator*
 Helen Sater, *Staff Assistant*

Memphis Convention Center Services
 David Greer, *Executive Manager*

Technical Planning

Glen Campbell, *Coordinator*

Catalogue Production
  Nancy E. Bogatin, *Project Manager*
  Dr. Rita E. Freed, *Author*
  Liz Conway, *Editor*
  Carol Lynn Yellin, *Consulting Editor*
  Polly Sexton, *Designer*
  Jon Abbott, *Photographer*
  William Eggleston, *Photographer*
  Kenneth S. Graetz, *Photographer*
  Lynn Gipson, *Technical Editor*
  Anna Kay Walker, *Technical Editor*
  Marcol Graphics of Memphis,
    R. Stoots, *Typography*
  St. Luke's Press, *Distributor*
  Lithograph Printing Company,
    Production and Printing
    Herbert (Dutch) Akers
    Russ Gordon
    Sheila Hudson

Exhibition Construction
  Richard Hudson, *Manager*
  Clark Eden, *Assistant Manager*
  Brian Foshee, *Architect Engineer*
  Engineering Management Construction,
    General Contractors
  Rathe Productions, *Case Construction*

Object Packing and Installation
  Andre Chenue & Fils Internationaux

Ground Transportation
  Lanigan Storage and Van Lines

Air Transportation
  Southern Air Transport

Equipment and Rigging
  Acuff Crane and Rigging
Hanger Space and Air Freight Movement
  Tennessee Air National Guard

Insurance
  Jean Markowitz

Security
  Captain Joe Holt, *Manager*
  Lt. Hudson Brown, *Assistant Manager*
  Lt. Billy J. Middleton, *Assistant Manager*
  Lt. D. E. Brewer, *Assistant Manager*
  Ben Hale, *Consultant*
  Guardsmark, Inc., *Consultant*

Financial Administration

Robert Tamboli, *Coordinator*

  Phil Botto, *Assistant Coordinator*
  Don Morris, *Audit Manager*
  Glenn Foster, *Cash Control*
  Marie Owens, *Auditing*
  Cassandra Taylor, *Auditing*
  Jane Umfress, *Budget*
  Arthur Anderson Company, *Consultant*
  Martha Sugg, *Advisor*

Communications

Jack Kyle, *Coordinator*

  John Malmo Advertising
  Memphis Convention and Visitors Bureau
  Tennessee Department of Tourist
    Development
  Perran Howell
  Floyd H. Fulkerson
  Brenda Mitchell
  Bernice Tutterow

Ticket Administration and Group Sale

Twyla Dixon, *Coordinator*

  Rochelle Gold, *Assistant Coordinator*
  Ticketmaster, *Ticket Sales*

Contributors

The Organizing Committee wishes to express appreciation to the following individuals and organizations for their generous support of the Ramesses The Great Exhibition.

Onnig G. Alixanian
American Embassy, Cairo, Egypt
American Institute of Architects,
    Memphis Chapter
American Women in Radio & Television,
    Memphis Chapter
Amtrak
Argenbright, Inc.
Askew, Nixon, Ferguson & Wolf, Inc.
Phil Barksdale
Phyllis Bell
Edward Marshall Boehm, Inc.
Judy Boshwit
Charles Chandler
Crowne Plaza
Metcalf Crump
Robert Crump's Hancock House
Delta Life and Annuity
Dr. Mursi Saad El-Din
Embassy of Egypt
Embassy of Egypt,
    Office of Press and Information
Chuck Engelkin
Pat Fleming
Wendy Fogelman
James H. Frantz
Foster Auto World
Goldsmith's Department Store
Goodyear Blimp
Great River Carnival
Peggy Hancock
Roger Knox
John A. Lindburg
Madison Cadillac
McDonald's

Memphis Area Chamber of Commerce
Memphis Arts Council
Memphis Caravan
Memphis City Schools—
    Vocal Music Department
Memphis Light, Gas, and Water Division
Memphis Symphony Orchestra
Memphis State University Concert Band
Methodist Health Systems
Mid-American Arabian Horse
    Association
Mockbee, Coker, Howorth Architects
Naegale Outdoor Advertising Company
    of Memphis
National Council of Jewish Women
National Endowment for the Arts
Naval Air Station Memphis
Organ Guild of Memphis
Kate Pera
Pryor Oldsmobile
Quaker Oats
State Information Service of Egypt
Tennessee Air National Guard
Bob Thieman
U.S. Army Herald Trumpets
U.S. Department of State
U.S. Information Agency
U.S. Navy Band-Millington
U.S. Naval Technical Training Center
United Wines
University of Tennessee-Memphis
Nick Vergos
Frank Ward
Don Wright
Xerox

Principal Sponsors

Coca-Cola USA

EgyptAir

Federal Express Corporation

First Tennessee

Holiday Inns, Inc.-Hotel Group

Malone & Hyde, Inc.

Northwest Airlines

A Statement from the Executive Director of the Ramesses the Great Exhibition

From ancient Memphis on the beautiful Nile to modern Memphis on the mighty Mississippi—it is an honor and a pleasure to welcome the majestic splendor of ancient Egypt.

There can be no finer example of community spirit and cooperation than that which is responsible for this presentation. From Mrs. Rudi Scheidt's personal quest of a beautiful dream for her city to Mayor Richard Hackett's tenacious and aggressive pursuit of that dream—from the forthright and up-front support of our corporate community to the dramatic resolve of the City Council, the Ramesses The Great Exhibition is truly a presentation by and for the people of Memphis and the Mid-South.

The unique opportunity to share this experience with the Egyptian Antiquities Organization, under the expert direction of Dr. Ahmed Kadry, has been a rare opportunity which will never be forgotten. The advice and counsel of Dr. Gammal Mohktar and the assistance and support of the entire antiquities committee have been most meaningful in the planning process. Those friendships will be treasured forever.

The success of the Exhibition is due in large measure to the gracious assistance of Egyptian Ambassador El Sayed Abdel Raouf El Reedy and his capable staff. We also owe a debt of gratitude to Ambassador Frank Wisner and the fine staff of the American Embassy in Cairo.

I want to acknowledge the efforts of the Egyptian Ministry of Culture, the United States Department of State, the United States Information Agency, the National Endowment for the Arts, and Congressman Donald Sundquist for the important roles they played in the success of the project.

Of course, this presentation would not have been possible without the dedication of our many loyal volunteers under the general direction of the Junior League of Memphis. Sincere appreciation is also extended to the Division Directors of the City of Memphis and their fine employees as well as to the management and staff of the Memphis Convention Center.

Finally, I want to very personally and sincerely thank my executive staff for making the impossible a reality. They alone can appreciate the monumental task which has been accomplished and they alone can savor the memories of that effort.

James E. Broughton
Executive Director
RAMESSES THE GREAT EXHIBITION

Statement from Memphis Brooks Museum of Art

Memphis Brooks Museum of Art is honored to participate in the presentation of *Ramesses the Great* in Memphis, Tennessee.

The impetus for the Memphis presentation originated during a 1984 visit to Cairo by Rudi Scheidt, a Museum trustee, with his wife, Helen (Honey). After learning from Dr. Mohamed Saleh, Director General of the Egyptian Museum in Cairo, of early plans for this exhibition to travel to Canada, Honey asked, "Why not Memphis as well?" She contacted Memphis Mayor Richard C. Hackett whose continuing efforts and determined negotiations transformed the dream into reality. Museum trustee support for this exhibition continues at a high level. Nancy E. Bogatin, chairman, has personally and professionally devoted countless hours to the exhibition and its development.

Memphis Brooks is the coordinator of the artistic and educational components of the exhibition. The installation design was created by George Sexton Associates. They have sensitively located the Ramesses art objects within the architectural environment of an Egyptian temple. Their concepts and enthusiasm have been crucial to the success of this project. The installation is complemented by this distinctive catalogue, written by Dr. Rita Freed, Director of the Institute of Egyptian Art and Archaeology, Memphis State University. The design of the catalogue conveys the scale and grandeur of this exhibition and of the great pharaoh, Ramesses II.

Educational programs structured by Patricia Bladon, Museum Curator of Education, have been the most extensive ever undertaken by an arts organization in the Mid-South. A teacher/student catalogue and detailed lesson plans have been produced for distribution through area school systems. As chairperson of the Ramesses Education Committee, she and her staff have worked in conjunction with dedicated volunteers and prepared audio/video programs and disseminated information about Ramesses the Great. Through Memphis State University's Institute of Egyptian Art and Archaeology, Anna Kay Walker, Co-Chairperson of the Ramesses Education Committee, was instrumental in helping to execute and administer these varied programs. Mary Scheuner of Christian Brothers College and Dr. Stephen McKenzie of Rhodes College conducted extensive research for special interest symposia. The goal of the Ramesses Education Committee has been to ensure that the exhibition makes a lasting impact on this city with its long-standing ties to Egypt.

Ramesses was a great builder. Perhaps he would appreciate that, as his exhibition is presented at the Memphis Convention Center, construction has begun on a major renovation and expansion at Memphis Brooks Museum of Art. Support for this expansion has, like that for this exhibition, been inspired by the perceptive vision of Mayor Richard C. Hackett.

Recognition of the critical role of the arts in the life of modern Memphis has been a priority of his administration. It is all the more appropriate, then, that an exhibition celebrating Ramesses the Great opens in Memphis at this time of enlightened joint effort by the city's leadership.

J. Richard Gruber
Director, Memphis Brooks Museum of Art

Statement from the Institute of Egyptian Art and Archaeology

Warrior, statesman, builder, family man, and possibly pharaoh of the Exodus, Ramesses the Great ruled over 3,000 years ago when Egypt's empire was at its peak. Since so many of the monuments visible in Memphis, Egypt today bear his name, it is entirely fitting that the treasures of this great king come to Memphis, Tennessee. Thanks to the vision of the leaders of the two great modern cultures involved, the study of a wonderful ancient civilization has led to a deep international friendship. The Institute of Egyptian Art and Archaeology of Memphis State University is proud to join the City of Memphis, the Egyptian Antiquities Organization, and the Memphis Brooks Museum of Art in sponsoring this exhibition.

Established in 1984, the Institute of Egyptian Art and Archaeology evolved out of the interest generated in our city by a collection of Egyptian antiquities housed in the Memphis State University Gallery. Its aims are to exhibit Egyptian art, to participate in the excavations of ancient Memphis, to teach the civilization of ancient Egypt both to the University community and the general public, and to conduct research. In 1985, it was designated as a Center of Excellence by the State of Tennessee.

The success of its programs is due in large measure to the enthusiastic involvement of its Board of Governors, especially Chairman Jack Kyle and the Memphis State University administration led by President Thomas G. Carpenter. The Institute of Egyptian Art and Archaeology is especially grateful to Mrs. Rudi Scheidt, who was both instrumental in the Institute's establishment and who has served from the start as a member of its Board of Governors. Her knowledge and foresight helped secure this splendid exhibition for Memphis, Tennessee. Persisting long after others would have given up, a member of the Institute's Honorary Board of Governors, Memphis Mayor Richard C. Hackett, overcame seemingly insurmountable obstacles to see this project through. By power of example, both of these Memphians have demonstrated that we are limited only by our dreams.

The extensive educational program of the Ramesses The Great Exhibition is the product of a unique cooperation between the Institute of Egyptian Art and Archaeology and Memphis Brooks Museum of Art. Co-chairwoman of the Education Committee Anna Kay Walker and advisor Dr. Edward Bleiberg of the Institute worked closely with Patricia Bladon of Memphis Brooks to insure that information about the exhibition's rare cultural treasures would reach students ages five to 105.

Another aspect of Egyptian Institute's educational and curatorial role may be seen in the exhibition's catalogue. It also provides yet another example of cooperation between cultural institutions. The Egyptian Antiquities Organization supplied otherwise unobtainable photographs and permission to include unpublished material. Memphis Brooks Museum of Art coordinated the catalogue's editing and technical production.

It is hoped that this catalogue will both enhance the experience of the public in viewing the exhibition and serve as a lasting reminder of this splendid culture long after the objects themselves have returned to the land of their origin. For, as historians have recognized since antiquity, through the enlightened understanding of our past, we are better able to contemplate our future.

Rita E. Freed
Director, Institute of Egyptian Art and Archaeology

Acknowledgements

Ramesses the Great's empire succeeded and endured because of the participation and support of many. So, too, is this catalogue of his exploits and world the product of the ideas and assistance of Egyptologists and others from around the world. Its creation is the brainchild of the City of Memphis, especially Mayor Richard C. Hackett and Executive Director of the Exhibition and the City's Chief Administrative Officer, James E. Broughton. It has enjoyed the enthusiastic cooperation of the Egyptian Antiquities Organization, especially its former President, Dr. Gamal Mokhtar.

The catalogue attempts to recount the story of the life of Egypt's great King Ramesses II and his world to the interested lay public. Subjects discussed in the essay and their relative order reflect the nature and arrangement of the objects in the exhibition.

For sharing his expertise, I am especially grateful to Dr. Kenneth A. Kitchen of the University of Liverpool. The dates cited for events in the life of Ramesses the Great and his officials conform to Kitchen's chronology. For providing many new insights and for giving generously of their time to ensure the accuracy and completeness of this manuscript, I am indebted to James B. Manning of New York and Memphis State University, Richard Fazzini of The Brooklyn Museum, Bernard V. Bothmer of the Institute of Fine Arts of New York University, and Peter Shapiro of New York. Additionally, I wish to thank my colleagues Janine Bourriau, Susan K. Doll, Zahi Hawass, Cathleen Keller and John McIntire.

For not only granting me access to their photographic archives and research libraries but also for making me feel at home therein, I am grateful additionally to the following institutions and individuals: Center of Documentation and Studies on Ancient Egypt (C.E.D.A.E.), especially Dr. Abdel-Aziz Sadek; the Department of Egyptian, Classical and Ancient Middle Eastern Art and Wilbour Library of The Brooklyn Museum, especially, Dr. Robert S. Bianchi, James F. Romano, Dr. Ogden Goelet, Vicki Solia, and Diane Guzman; the Department of Egyptian and Ancient Near Eastern Art of the Museum of Fine Arts, Boston, especially Dr. Edward Brovarski, Peter Lacovara, Sue D'Auria, Catharine A. Roehrig, Dr. Timothy Kendall and Peter der Manuelian; the Department of Egyptian Art of the Metropolitan Museum of Art, especially Dr. Christine Lilyquist and Marsha Hill; the National Geographic Society, especially Dori Babyak; and Barbara Shattuck, and the Manning/Pleskow Archive in New York.

The majority of the excellent photographs of Ramesside monuments included here are the work of Jon Abbott, who, with his assistant Anne Edgerton, accompanied me in the footsteps of Ramesses II from Qantir to Abu Simbel during the dog days of July. For their courage and persistance, I am especially grateful. Credit for the ease with which our work was accomplished belongs to the Egyptian Antiquities Organization, especially Dr. Gamal Mokhtar, Dr. Ahmed Kadry, Dr. Mohamed Saleh, Galal Sharawy, Abdin Siam and Rada ali Soliman.

Also present with me in Egypt was world-renowned photographer William Eggleston, on assignment for Memphis Brooks Museum of Art. He and Memphis Brooks have generously allowed a selection of his work to be included here as an introductory photographic essay.

For their kindness in supplying previously unpublished excavation material, I am grateful to the following expeditions: the Egypt Exploration Society Memphis Project, especially Professor H.S. Smith and David Jeffreys; the joint Egypt Exploration Society-Rijksmuseum van Oudheden, Leiden Expedition to the New Kingdom Necropolis at Saqqara, especially Geoffrey T. Martin; the Qantir Expedition of the Pelizaeus-Museum, Hildesheim, especially Dr. Edgar Pusch; The Brooklyn Museum Mut Expedition, especially Richard Fazzini and Mary McKercher; and the Wadi Tumilat Project of the University of Toronto, especially Phyllis and John S. Holladay, Jr.

To all those involved in its production, this catalogue was more than just a job. For their personal concern, and hard work, special thanks are due technical planning coordinator Glen Campbell, catalogue project coordinator Nancy E. Bogatin, editor Liz Conway, consulting editor Carol Lynn Yellin, index compiler Catherine C. Swearingen, and contributing editor Valerie Moore.

Dedicated assistant Lynn Gipson and IEAA Curator of Education Anna Kay Walker helped in a myriad way at all hours, often at a moment's notice. In this regard, I wish also to thank Emily Sharp, Edward Orio, Diane Reed, Jane Jarvi, Elizabeth Powell, James R. Wagner and Lucia Burch, as well as typists Kipp Williams, Brenda Landman, Betty Leigh Hutcheson and Nancy Douglass.

The richness of color reproduction and attractive appearance of the catalogue is due in large measure to the uncompromising standards and generosity of Lithograph Printing Company, especially Vice President Herbert "Dutch" Akers, Mike Hines and Sheila Hudson, as well as Ronnie Stoots and the staff of Marcol Graphics.

For granting me time to work on the catalogue, and, as always, for their support and encouragement, I thank Dr. Richard R. Ranta, Dean of the College of Communication and Fine Arts of Memphis State University, Dr. Carol J. Crown, Chairman of its Department of Art, and my colleague at the Institute of Egyptian Art and Archaeology, Dr. Edward Bleiberg.

To all these individuals and institutions, a sincere "thank you" for helping to make this catalogue all we wanted it to be.

R.E.F.

Egyptian Chronology

PREDYNASTIC PERIOD
(4000-3200 B.C.)
Communal settlements. Domestication of animals and plants. Decorated pottery, flint tools, slate palettes, jewelry buried with dead in individual graves in cemeteries.

 Badarian
 Amratian (Nagada I)
 Gerzean (Nagada II)

EARLY DYNASTIC I-II
(3200-2780 B.C.)
Unification of Upper and Lower Egypt. Formative period for architecture, art, language.

Dynasty I: 3200-2980 B.C.
Dynasty II: 2980-2780 B.C.

OLD KINGDOM III-VI
(2780-2258 B.C.)
Pyramid Age. King as manifestation of god on earth and absolute authority. Rise of sun cult. Memphis as center of politics, art, learning. Classical age for art.

Dynasty III: 2780-2680 B.C.
Dynasty IV: 2680-2565 B.C.
Dynasty V: 2565-2420 B.C.
Dynasty VI: 2420-2258 B.C.

FIRST INTERMEDIATE PERIOD VII-X
(2258-2052 B.C.)
Dissolution of central monarchy. Usurpation of power by provincial leaders. Decline in art styles.

Dynasty VII: Interregnum
Dynasty VIII (Memphite):
 2258-2232 B.C.
Dynasty IX (Heracleopolitan):
 2232-2140 B.C.
Dynasty X (Heracleopolitan):
 2140-2052 B.C.

MIDDLE KINGDOM XI-XII
(2134-1786 B.C.)
Reunification of Egypt and reestablishment of central monarchy. King as careworn good shepherd. Rise of cult of Osiris. Democratization of religious beliefs. Classical age for language.

Dynasty XI: 2134-1991 B.C.
Dynasty XII: 1991-1786 B.C.

SECOND INTERMEDIATE PERIOD XIII-XVII
(1786-1570 B.C.)
Again dissolution of central monarchy. Hyksos invade from the east.

Dynasties XIII-XIV: 1786-1680 B.C.
 about thirty kings partly contemporaneous
Dynasties XV-XVI: 1720-1570 B.C.
 Hyksos in north; local rulers in Thebes
Dynasty XVII: 1600-1570 B.C.

NEW KINGDOM XVIII-XX
(1570-1085 B.C.)
Expulsion of Hyksos and conquest of empire to south and east. Amun as national god. Theban temples amass vast wealth. Akhenaten and wife Nefertiti renounce cult of Amun and establish the sun disk as sole god. Capital moves to Amarna. Naturalism in art. Tutankhamun restores old religion and moves back to Thebes.

Dynasty XVIII: 1570-1314 B.C.
 Ahmose I
 Amunhotep I
 Tuthmosis I
 Tuthmosis II
 Hatshepsut
 Tuthmosis III
 Amunhotep II
 Tuthmosis IV
 Amunhotep III
 Akhenaten
 Semenkhkare
 Tut-ankh-amun
 Ay
 Horemheb
Dynasty XIX: 1314-1197 B.C.
 Ramesses I
 Sety I
 Ramesses II
 Merneptah
 Amunmesse
 Sety II
 Siptah (Merneptah)
 Tausert
Dynasty XX: 1197-1085 B.C.
 Seth-nakht
 Ramesses III
 Ramesses IV-Ramesses XI

THIRD INTERMEDIATE PERIOD XXI-XXIV
(1085-715 B.C.)
Authority divided between powerful priesthood at Thebes and ruling family in Delta.

Dynasty XXI (Tanis and Thebes):
 1085-950 B.C.

Dynasty XXII (Bubastite):
 950-730 B.C.
Dynasty XXIII: 817 (?)-730 B.C.
 Six kings contemporaneous with the end of Dynasty XXII
Dynasty XXIV: 730-715 B.C.

LATE PERIOD XXV-XXXI
(730-332 B.C.)
Alternation between foreign and native rulers. Artistic revival. Development of true portraiture.

Dynasty XXV (Kushite):
 730-656 B.C.
Assyrian invasion:
 Esarhaddon captures Memphis:
 671 B.C.
 Ashurbanipal sacks Thebes:
 663 B.C.
Dynasty XXVI (Saite): 664-525 B.C.
Persian invasion under Cambyses:
 525 B.C.
Dynasty XXVII: First Persian
 Domination:
 525-404 B.C.
Dynasties XXVIII-XXIX:
 404-378 B.C.
 Six kings maintain independence against Persia
Dynasty XXX: 378-341 B.C.
Dynasty XXXI: Second Persian
 Domination: 341-332 B.C.
Conquest of Alexander: 332 B.C.

MACEDONIAN KINGS
(331-304 B.C.)
Conquest by Alexander the Great

PTOLEMAIC DYNASTY
(304-30 B.C.)
Establishment of Greek ruling family. Extensive temple building. Mixture of Greek and Egyptian styles.

ROMAN PERIOD
(30 B.C.-A.D. 640)
Conquest by Augustus Caesar. Exploitation for Roman Empire. Egyptian cults forbidden by edict of Constantine. Conversion to Christianity.

ISLAMIC PERIOD
(A.D. 640 to present)
Conquest by Muslims and conversion to Islam.

Adapted from W.S. Smith, *The Art and Architecture of Ancient Egypt*, revised with additions by W.K. Simpson (Middlesex, England: Penguin, 1981).

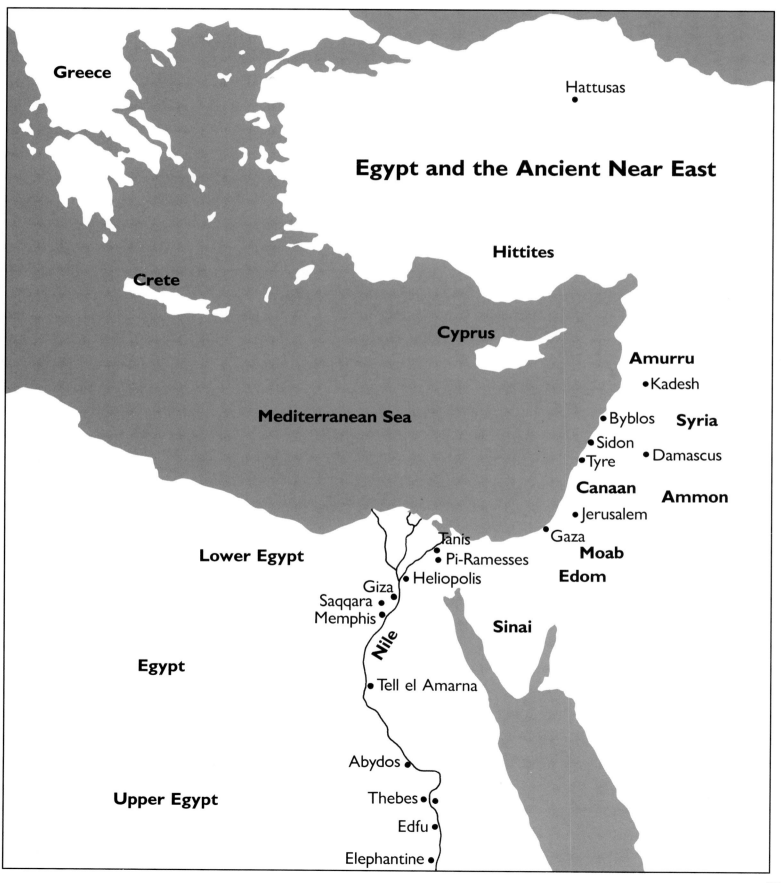

Greece

Hattusas

Egypt and the Ancient Near East

Hittites

Crete

Cyprus

Amurru

• Kadesh

Mediterranean Sea

• Byblos   **Syria**

• Sidon

• Damascus

• Tyre

Canaan   **Ammon**

• Jerusalem

Lower Egypt   Tanis   Gaza

• Pi-Ramesses   **Moab**

• Heliopolis   **Edom**

Giza •

Saqqara •

Memphis •   **Sinai**

Egypt   Nile

• Tell el Amarna

Abydos •

Upper Egypt   Thebes • •

• Edfu

Elephantine •

xxiii

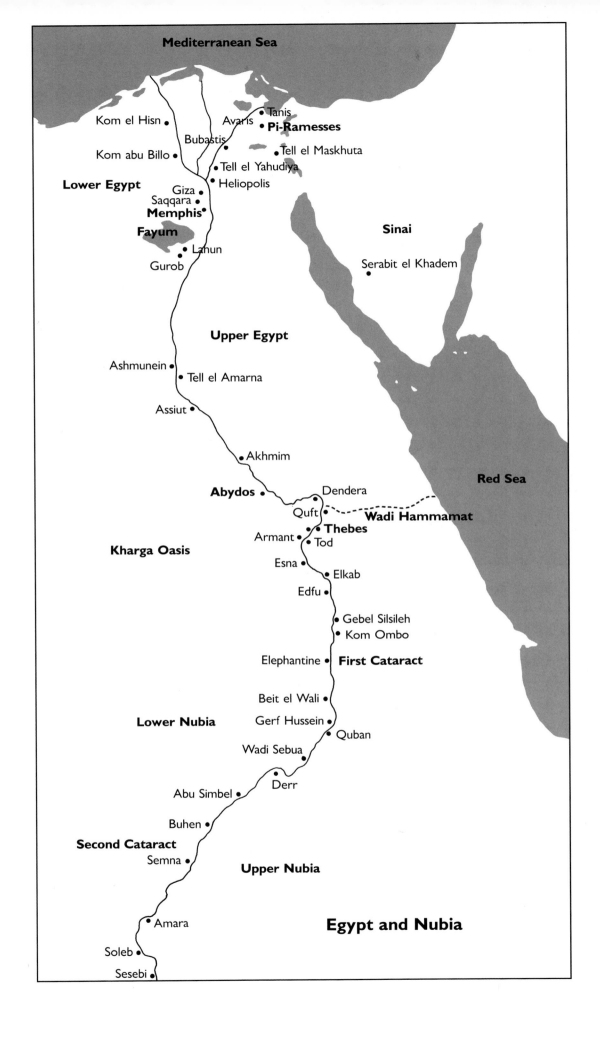

Mediterranean Sea

Kom el Hisn
Avaris
Tanis
Pi-Ramesses
Bubastis
Tell el Maskhuta
Kom abu Billo
Tell el Yahudiya
Lower Egypt
Heliopolis
Giza
Saqqara
Memphis
Fayum
Lahun
Gurob

Sinai

Serabit el Khadem

Upper Egypt

Ashmunein
Tell el Amarna

Assiut

Akhmim

Red Sea

Dendera
Abydos
Quft
Wadi Hammamat
Armant
Thebes
Tod
Kharga Oasis
Esna
Elkab
Edfu
Gebel Silsileh
Kom Ombo
Elephantine
First Cataract

Beit el Wali
Lower Nubia
Gerf Hussein
Quban
Wadi Sebua
Derr
Abu Simbel
Buhen
Second Cataract
Semna
Upper Nubia

Amara
Soleb
Sesebi

Egypt and Nubia

The Colossus of Memphis

Skillfully carved in granite from Aswan, the 24 foot, seven inch tall colossus journeyed 600 miles down river to Memphis, the glorious capital of ancient Egypt. Almighty Ramesses, pharaoh with dominion over Egypt's empire, would live forever in stone.

Ramesses the Great, identified by name on both the belt of his pleated royal kilt and on the statue's base, appears as he wished the world to remember him. He strides forward regally, left foot first in the traditional pose of Egyptian male figures. His arms hang at his sides, and in his right fist he clasps a folded bolt of cloth. The white crown of Upper Egypt (Nile Valley) rests on his head, and a long straight beard anchored to his chin with a strap further proclaims his royal status. Jewels adorn his strong neck and powerful wrists, and a dagger hangs from his belt. Ramesses' figure is youthfully trim, and his noble countenance was rendered with particular care.

Ramesses dedicated this colossus to Ptah, the patron god of Memphis. It flanked one of the small temples along the processional way leading to the main south gate of the sacred enclosure of the temple of Ptah. Perhaps, it stood beside a companion statue of similar scale wearing the Lower Egyptian (Delta) crown.

Other kings before and after erected colossal statues of themselves, but none are larger in size or greater in number than the ones commissioned by Ramesses the Great. Throughout Egypt and Nubia, these colossi stood like guardians beside temple facades or inside open temple courts. By their magnitude and their presence on sacred temple grounds, the statues provided tangible and awe inspiring reminders of the earthly power of Ramesses the Great and of his closeness to the gods. These statues embodied both the essence of kingship and divinity. They functioned as intermediaries between the people of Egypt and the inaccessible gods inside the

Conservators moved the Colossus of Memphis in preparation for restoration.

Restoration of the Colossus of Memphis was conducted on site, only yards away from where the statue had been buried for centuries!

Ramsy Nageeb served as architect on the project. Abd Allah el Hossany and Hamdiny held the positions of chief restorers.

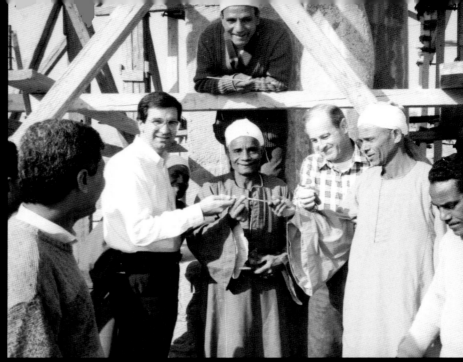

In appreciation for his role in making the restoration possible, Memphis Mayor Richard C. Hackett received tools actually used on the project.

temples. Passers-by delivering petitions and prayers relied on Ramesses the Great to intercede with the gods on their humble behalf.

Ramesses the Great erected at least ten other larger than life statues of himself in the vicinity of the temple of Ptah. Although only fragments of most remain, two others have survived the centuries and are among Egypt's finest and most famous monuments. One stands in front of Cairo's bustling railroad station at an intersection known as Ramesses Square. The other lies in its own open-air museum near where it once stood in ancient Memphis.

At an unknown time in history and by perpetrators unidentified, a heavy blunt instrument reduced the great Colossus of Memphis to ruin. This once splendid statue fell on its left side and wind-blown earth covered it.

For centuries, Ramesses' colossus was lost to the world. In 1962 it was rediscovered behind the present open-air museum by machinery digging the foundation for a restaurant. Construction immediately stopped, and the statue's three largest pieces were moved onto wood pilings to prevent further ravages by the elements. Thus, through the colossus, Ramesses regained his place as a commanding presence in ancient Memphis.

In early 1986, after visiting Memphis, Egypt, delegations led by Mayor Richard C. Hackett of Memphis, Tennessee, recognized the beauty and significance of these magnificent ruins and requested that the Egyptian Antiquities Organization include the Colossus of Memphis in the Memphis showing of the *Ramesses the Great* exhibition. Egyptian officials agreed, and consultations with international art experts commenced. Coca-Cola USA generously offered to fund the project, and restoration began on the statue in Memphis, Egypt, during June of 1986. When the Denver Museum of Natural History learned of Memphis' efforts, they offered to participate in the restoration project.

Approximately 30 conservators worked 16 hours daily through January 1987 to reassemble the three large pieces and many smaller fragments. Steel pins were added for stability and strength. Artisans reconstructed the missing knee area of the right leg, right foot and parts of the base, using powdered granite, poured concrete and steel rods. A back slab, added for increased support, replaced a smaller back pillar. The restored colossus now weighs 47 tons.

In preparation for its journey to Memphis on the Mississippi, Lloyd's of London insured the precious treasure. Conservators disassembled the statue into three pieces and packed it into wooden crates (adding yet another four tons!). An Egyptian army honor guard escorted the heavy transport trucks which took the colossus from Memphis, Egypt to Mediterranean shores at Alexandria. There, under the close supervision of Antiquities Organization officials, the wooden crates were packed in a steel case and placed aboard the *Aquila*. A military band and a naval escort into international waters provided a befitting royal send-off as the colossus departed for the port of Marseilles, France on February 5, 1987. The colossus' incredible journey continued as it was transferred to the *Express* for its Atlantic crossing bound for Savannah, Georgia. It arrived on U.S. shores in late February, and early in March, two huge trucks caravaned to the Memphis Convention Center.

To accommodate the colossus of Ramesses the Great, tiles had to be removed from the Memphis Convention Center's 38 foot ceiling. A 45 ton forklift and 50 ton crane, supplied by Acuff Crane and Rigging Company, reassembled the statue on a steel girded weight distribution platform.

The statue which once stood as temple guardian and petitioner of the gods now stands as the focal point of the *Ramesses the Great* exhibition in Memphis where it bridges thousands of years and thousands of miles. The statue of the great petitioner was petitioned for, and restored by, a remarkable cooperative effort led by Mayor Richard C. Hackett, the City of Memphis, Tennessee, the Egyptian Antiquities Organization, the Denver Museum of Natural History and the generosity of Coca-Cola USA.

The colossus inspired awe then, and it inspires awe now. Ramesses has seen Memphis in ancient Egypt and Memphis in the 20th century United States. Today, it serves as a symbol of cooperation between two great countries, and it will continue to stand as a timeless testimony to the power of international friendship.

With restoration almost completed, the Colossus of Memphis once again assumes its proper position.

7

Ramesses the Great's Colossus: from Ancient Memphis to Modern Memphis

1279-1213 B.C.	Ramesses the Great commissions a larger than life statue of himself to stand outside the Ptah Temple precinct at Memphis.
B.C.-A.D.	Ancient despoilers destroy the statue with heavy blunt instruments. Lying broken on its side, desert winds shift earth which eventually covers the colossus.
A.D. 1962	Egyptian construction workers unexpectedly make an important archaeological discovery! They find statue fragments while digging a foundation for a new restaurant.
1962-1984	Lack of funds precludes restoration of this once magnificent treasure.
December, 1984	Memphis, Tennessee, Mayor Richard C. Hackett leads a delegation to ancient Memphis and expresses interest in bringing the statue to Memphis, Tennessee.
February, 1985	*Ramesses the Great* exhibition officials visit Egypt and formally request permission from the Egyptian Antiquities Organization to include Ramesses' colossus in the Memphis exhibition.
	Egyptian Antiquities Organization informs Memphis that the statue must be restored before leaving its Egyptian homeland.
	Egyptian officials sign a letter of intent to include the statue as part of the Canadian and U.S. tour of the *Ramesses the Great* exhibition.
August, 1985	Egyptian officials sign *Ramesses the Great* exhibition contract minus provisions for the Colossus of Memphis. All parties understand that separate agreements must be reached to include the colossus.
January, 1986	James H. Franz of the Metropolitan Museum of Art, New York and Michael S. Fletcher, an engineer with the architectural firm Skidmore, Owings & Merrill, journey to Egypt and prepare feasibility study on the statue's restoration. The Memphis *Commercial Appeal* funds their study.

March/April, 1986	*Ramesses the Great* exhibition officials verbally agree to underwrite the Egyptian Antiquities Organization's $100,000 cost of restoring the Colossus of Memphis.
June, 1986	Although written agreement is not signed, restoration begins.
October, 1986	Statue contract signed between City of Memphis, Tennessee, and Egyptian Antiquities Organization. Denver Museum of Natural History agrees to share cost of statue restoration and transportation.
December, 1986	Jacques Gaudin of Maison Chenue of Paris, France, visits Egypt to arrange the packing and shipping of the colossus.
January, 1987	Largest statue restoration project ever undertaken by the Egyptian Antiquities Organization is completed. Conservators pack restored statue in three padded wooden crates. Heavy transport trucks with military honor guard carry the colossus from Memphis to Alexandria harbor. Original ship selected to transport the statue wrecks in the Mediterranean en route to Alexandria. New travel provisions are quickly arranged.
February, 1987	Colossus crates are placed in heavy steel container for protection on board the *M.V. Aquila*. Full military honors accompany the statue as it leaves the Alexandria harbor. The colossus of Ramesses the Great arrives in Marseilles, France. Its crates are transferred to the *Express* for the arduous Atlantic crossing. The *Express* sails for Savannah, Georgia with its priceless cargo. The Colossus of Memphis reaches American soil and is transferred to two trucks.
March, 1987	The colossus completes its journey from ancient Memphis to modern Memphis, Tennessee! Memphis' Acuff Crane and Rigging provides 45 ton forklift and 50 ton crane to install the Colossus of Memphis at the Memphis Convention Center.
April 15, 1987	*Ramesses the Great* exhibition opens in Memphis, Tennessee with the modern world premier showing of the Colossus of Memphis.
September, 1987	The Colossus of Memphis departs modern Memphis for exhibition at the Denver Museum of Natural History.
Post 1987	The Colossus of Memphis will permanently reside in the courtyard of the Museum of Civilization in Cairo as a testimony to international friendship.

Thanks to an international effort,
the Colossus of Memphis no longer
lies in ruin!

Eggleston's Egypt

The following eight pages contain works drawn from the *Egyptian Project Portfolio* by internationally known color photographer William Eggleston. During the summer of 1986, Eggleston journeyed to the lands of Ramesses the Great in an effort to capture a distinctive and fresh view of Egypt. These photographs accurately reflect in microcosm what resulted in Eggleston's *Egyptian Project.*

Memphis Brooks Museum of Art initiated and sponsored Eggleston's project which had no creative restraints or limitations in its commission. Consequently, he was afforded the rare luxury of approaching his assignment in the tradition of nineteenth century photographic expeditions. Before retracing the footsteps of Ramesses the Great, Eggleston joined Dr. Rita E. Freed in Cairo for an orientation to the land of the pharaohs. For three weeks, Eggleston surveyed Egypt's virtually limitless field of images with his vintage Leica camera. The photographs selected convey a sense of order and composition unique to Eggleston while they also accurately reflect what it is like to be in Egypt. Consequently, the images offer many layers of meaning to both casual viewers and to sophisticated students of fine photography.

Eggleston's Egypt in Microcosm

Ramesses the Great at Memphis, *pages 12-13.*

Avenue of rams at Karnak, *pages 14-15.*

Merneptah, son and successor of Ramesses the Great, *page 16.*

Ptah Temple Precinct at Memphis, *page 17.*

Deir el Bahari, near the final resting place of Ramesses the Great, *pages 18-19.*

Small temple of Ptah at Memphis, *page 20.*

I
Ramesses the King

The Nile at Gebel Silsileh.

Ramesses the Great wearing the warrior crown and holding the scepter of kingship.

E ach summer in ancient Egypt, the first appearance in the heavens of the Dog Star Sirius heralded the start of a crucial occurrence on earth: the annual flooding of the Nile. The river's waters would soon rise and, when they receded, leave behind a rich layer of fertile black silt, promising yet another year of high crop yields. Around 1317 B.C., a rare thing happened. When the bright star's first rising was observed on approximately July 19, the date marked the beginning of a new year for both the religious and civil calendars. This convergence took place only once every 1,461 years and was regarded, the divine chronicles relate, as an omen of great things soon to come on earth.

Less than 20 years later, around 1300 B.C., an infant destined to govern Egypt for more than six decades came into the world. This pharaoh-to-be, Ramesses II, was the son of the god Amun (who had assumed human form as King Sety I) and an earthly mother, Queen Tuya. In records he left of his own life, Ramesses II would later explain how it was evident almost immediately that his arrival on earth was the great event which had been forecast in the heavens. In that year of his birth, he would claim, record flood levels brought prosperity and joy to all the land.

Such confidence in his own destiny may have been justified. So numerous and impressive are the contemporary records—monumental, archaeological and literary— of his long reign and his many accomplishments, that history has recognized him as Ramesses the Great, the king whose name, in the thirteenth century B.C., inspired fear and awe throughout most of the known world. Because he became, quite literally, a legend in his own time, and because his name and reputation lived on in myth as well as history long after his death, Ramesses the Great unquestionably set a standard against which other rulers thereafter measured themselves and were measured by their own chroniclers.

The Nile's flood guaranteed the fertility of the land.

By honoring his ancestors
Ramesses II gave himself legitimacy.
A list of former kings is in the upper
registers. Below are the names of
Ramesses II. From Abydos.

A Pharaoh's Heritage

Young Ramesses (called Ramesses II, since his grandfather had also been named
Ramesses) was born into the prosperous world of the New Kingdom. It was Egypt's
Golden Age, when she was mistress of a wealthy empire. From his earliest years,
Ramesses was instructed by his father, King Sety I, about his own military family and
about Egypt's origins, her divine history and her long and impressive list of kings—
some 18 previous dynasties going back almost 2,000 years.

The New Kingdom had begun around 1550 B.C. with the reign of Ahmose, first
king of Dynasty XVIII. Ahmose not only expelled the Hyksos, foreign warrior groups
from Asia who had ruled Egypt for about 100 years, but also succeeded, from his
homeland in Thebes, in reunifying all of Egypt. Victory followed military victory, until
Egypt, under Ahmose's successors, had extended its borders to encompass all land
between the Fourth Cataract of the Nile in Nubia (Sudan) to northern Syria in the
Levant. The wealth of the newly conquered territories flowed into Egypt. Soldiers
returned laden with booty and captives, and foreign chieftains, eager to please their
new overlord, sent tribute. From Kush in the Sudan came quantities of gold, and from

yet farther south came rare woods, ivory, animal skins and precious unguents. Asiatic rulers sent Pharaoh precious stones, silver, timber, wines, spices, flowers and fruits for Egyptian gardens. Amun, the great god of Thebes, in whose name the empire had been conquered, received his share of the new-found riches, and his temple at Karnak became the wealthiest in the land.

Soon, a new cosmopolitan lifestyle developed as this rich variety of exotic raw materials and luxurious finished goods of foreign manufacture became available to the wealthy nobles and administrators who managed Egypt's internal affairs and governed her vast empire. Foreigners, arriving to trade in Egypt's ports or to settle in her bustling cities, brought with them their gods as well as their native customs. It was an age of great internationalism and economic vitality. Egypt thrived.

One Dynasty XVIII pharaoh who fully exploited Egypt's wealth and resources was King Amunhotep III. During his long peaceful reign, he embarked on a building program which both glorified Egypt's gods and elevated the king to a position of equal prominence. Colossal statues of Amunhotep III (which would inspire the future King Ramesses II) reminded passers-by of this divine power. His son and successor, however, reacting against the ever-increasing power of the priesthood of Amun, abandoned the old religion, shut down its temples and established the sun disk, the Aten, as the sole god. He changed his name from Amunhotep IV, meaning Amun-is-Satisfied, to Akhenaten, Blessed-Spirit-of-the-Aten or He-Who-Is-Beneficial-to-the-Aten, and erected a new capital city at the virgin site of Tell el Amarna in Middle Egypt. As the new religion's pontiff, Akhenaten worshiped the Aten in open-air shrines and honored his god with hymns which would later inspire Old Testament psalmists. During his 17-year rule, he also encouraged artistic freedom, instructing artists to represent the royal family in intimate poses with an unprecedented naturalism.

The period following Akhenaten's death was unsettled, and Dynasty XVIII drew to a close during the short and relatively ineffectual reigns of his successors, including the young Tutankhamun. Soon, the clergy of Amun set about restoring the old order with Thebes as the religious center and Amun as the chief god of the land. Egypt's rivals, seeing her resources sapped by religious turmoil and her energy focused on internal affairs, encouraged revolt in her conquered territories. When Tutankhamun passed on to the netherworld in 1331 B.C. without living offspring, his commander of chariotry, Ay, proclaimed himself Pharaoh. Upon his death four years later, he was succeeded by the general Horemheb, who also died without progeny.

In 1295 B.C., Paramessu, Horemheb's chief administrative officer and designated heir, proclaimed himself king as Ramesses (I). This former vizier, from a prominent military family of the Eastern Delta, thereby became the first king of Dynasty XIX and founder of the Ramesside royal house. Although Ramesses I ruled, at most, two years, monuments from Nubia to Canaan testify to his extensive building activity. When his son, Sety I, became ruler, he perpetuated his father's name by dedicating chapels to him in his own temples at Abydos and Gurna.

From the start, Sety I embarked on a program to restore Egypt's military authority. In Year 1 of his reign, he subdued cities in Canaan and southern Syria, returning them to Egyptian control. In Year 4 or 5, rumors of trouble on the western border prompted him to invade Libya. Beside him, now, was Prince Ramesses, his eldest son from his principal wife, Tuya, a boy in his early teens. Ramesses also accompanied his

Queen Tuya, mother of Ramesses II.

Sety I anoints his father Ramesses I
in the section of the Sety I funerary
temple at Gurna devoted to his
father's cult.

Paramessu, in a statue made before
he became king, wears the garment
of a vizier and holds a scribal palette.
From Karnak.

Ramesses the Great offers *Ma'at*, goddess of truth, to Ra-Horakhty. In return he receives life and power.

A superbly crafted colossal statue of Meryetamun, daughter and wife of Ramesses II, stood beside one of the king at a temple in Akhmim.

Colossal statue of Meryetamun *in situ*.

father the next year to Kadesh, a central Syrian city once under Egyptian sovereignty that had fallen to an invading Hittite force from the north. Sety I succeeded in entering Kadesh where he erected a stela (commemorative stone tablet), but the city later reverted to Hittite control. Years later, as Pharaoh, Ramesses would return to Kadesh.

Back in Egypt, Sety I turned his attention to domestic affairs, commissioning temples to Egypt's gods, celebrating their festivals and encouraging the exploitation of Egypt's natural resources. Here, too, starting about Year 7 of Sety I's rule, Prince Ramesses appeared beside his father in an official capacity, learning from him and acting as his deputy in administrative, military and religious affairs. Ramesses was probably still in his teens, although it would later be recorded that while yet ''in the egg'' he assumed responsibility for affairs of state.

The future kingship belonged (by divine right) to Prince Ramesses. His training included instruction in how to maintain divine order or balance in the universe, a concept known as *Ma'at*. When *Ma'at* was upheld, Egypt would prosper, the Nile would flood, her fields would produce high yields, and her enemies would remain subjugated. Let *Ma'at* be disturbed, and chaos would result.

In preparation for his future role, Prince Ramesses received the full royal titulary, five names expressing his divinity and linking him with his royal ancestors. Sety I selected beautiful women as a harem for his son, and young Ramesses began his own family. By the time he reached adulthood, he had already fathered many children by a number of wives.

Sety I ruled as long as 15 or 20 years, with Prince-Regent Ramesses at his side for at least half that time. When Sety died, Ramesses, a dutiful son, buried him in a large and splendid tomb in the Valley of the Kings, the royal necropolis on the west bank of the Nile at Thebes. Later, at Karnak on the east bank, at Gurna in Western Thebes and at Abydos in Middle Egypt, Ramesses II would finish his father's building projects, even commissioning a golden statue in honor of Sety I. (Of course, to make clear to the gods he had done so, he would carve his own name beside his father's or boast of his pious deeds in temple inscriptions.)

Builder of an Empire

The year was 1279 B.C. At sunrise on Day 27 of the Third month of *Shomu* (June), Ramesses II acceded to the throne. The coronation may have taken place in Memphis, the political and administrative capital located at the juncture of Upper and Lower Egypt (the Nile Valley and the Delta). Alternatively, it could have taken place in the sacred city of Heliopolis, slightly north of Memphis.

From the gods Ramesses received the crowns of Upper and Lower Egypt and accepted the crook and flail of rulership. A uraeus, or symbolic cobra, was placed upon his brow to protect him and destroy his enemies. Thus, the transfer of power was made, *Ma'at* restored and the threat of chaos averted. Ramesses II became the new Horus, the god incarnate.

The new pharaoh's royal names were then inscribed for eternity on the leaves of the sacred *ished* tree of Heliopolis (Cat. No. 5), thereby assuring Ramesses II millions of years of rule. Uncaged birds flew in all directions, and his five-part titulary was

By inscribing his names on the leaves of the *ished* tree, the gods grant Ramesses the Great eternal life and rule. From the Ramesseum.

proclaimed throughout the land:

> *The Horus:* Strong Bull, Beloved of *Ma'at*
> *He of the Two Goddesses:* Protector of Egypt who Subdues the
> Foreign Lands
> *The Golden Horus:* Rich in Years, Great in Victories
> *The King of Upper and Lower Egypt:* Strong in Right
> is Ra *(User-Ma'at-Ra)*
> *Son of Ra:* Ramesses, Beloved of Amun

The last two of his names, his prenomen *(User-Ma'at-Ra)* and nomen (Ramesses), were written in cartouches, encircling ovals which protected them and set them apart from the profane world. They signified the king's mastery over all that the sun shone upon. By Year 2 of his reign, *Setep-en-Ra* (Chosen of Ra) would be added to Ramesses II's prenomen, and, later, additional laudatory epithets would further proclaim his grandeur.

In his mid-twenties, when he became king, Ramesses II was about five and one-half feet tall and had auburn hair, a rather pronounced aquiline nose and a jutting chin. His ears had been pierced in childhood. Ancient Egyptian artisans, in keeping with the traditional canon of proportion, represented him with a perfectly formed body—square shoulders, a powerful chest, trim waist and bulging muscles in his arms and legs.

Ambitious, energetic and politically astute, Ramesses II began immediately to demonstrate his power and leave his stamp on the land. Evidence exists, dating from the earliest years of his long rule, of Ramesses the Great's construction activity at numerous sites throughout Egypt and Nubia. In just the first years of his reign, he initiated or augmented building projects at Abydos, Karnak, Luxor, Beit el Wali, Abu Simbel and elsewhere. He also erected stelae as far away as Sinai and Syria.

Within two months after his coronation, Ramesses II headed south to Thebes. This religious center would be a focus of attention throughout his rule, as it had been for earlier pharaohs whose funerary temples and tombs occupied the west bank. Nicknamed *Niwt,* ''The City,'' Thebes was a large urban center. Here, the vizier of Upper Egypt, chief administrator of the southern half of Egypt (see Cat. No. 33), made his headquarters and maintained governmental archives. As the homeland of the New Kingdom's most powerful gods, who lived primarily on the river's east bank where the sun rose and where life began, Thebes was also a divine city. Karnak, the home of Amun and other gods, was Egypt's largest and wealthiest temple, and Thebes had largely grown up around the temple to meet its needs. Since much of the city today lies buried under modern Luxor, its layout, industries and domestic areas remain largely unexplored.

Ramesses arrived on Day 25 of the Second month of *Akhet* (August) to take part in the Opet Festival. This was a time of great celebration, when the cult image of the god Amun visited the nearby Luxor temple so that he might be regenerated. Luxor, like a number of other sacred sites, claimed to be the site of the creation of the world, and the Opet Festival celebrated the precise moment of creation. As the god was regenerated, so too was an aspect of the soul of the new king, his *ka,* renewed through a re-creation of his divine conception and birth. For three weeks, a general carnival atmosphere prevailed. Singers, dancers, acrobats, sellers of food and drink,

The names of Ramesses II on the back of his statue from Tanis.

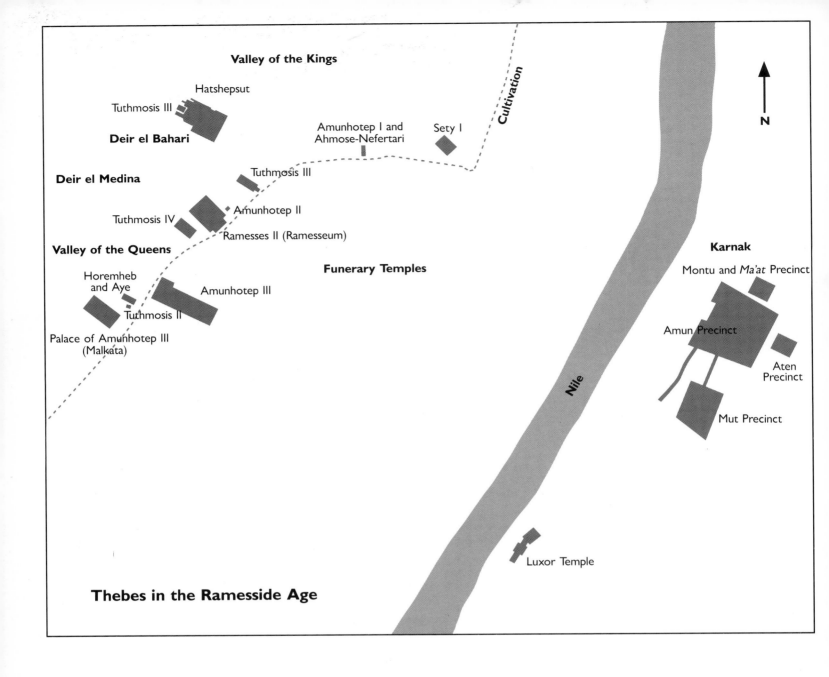

Valley of the Kings

Hatshepsut

Tuthmosis III

Deir el Bahari

Amunhotep I and
Ahmose-Nefertari

Sety I

Cultivation

N

Deir el Medina

Tuthmosis III

Amunhotep II

Tuthmosis IV

Ramesses II (Ramesseum)

Valley of the Queens

Funerary Temples

Karnak

Montu and *Ma'at* Precinct

Horemheb
and Aye

Amunhotep III

Amun Precinct

Aten
Precinct

Tuthmosis II

Palace of Amunhotep III
(Malkata)

Mut Precinct

Nile

Thebes in the Ramesside Age

Luxor Temple

A lithe acrobat performs a
backbend. Carnival-like activities
accompanied the Opet Festival.

and souvenir hawkers provided entertainment for all. At the end, when Amun returned to his home at Karnak, Ramesses II left Thebes secure in his new role as divine king. After his visit, the king demonstrated his gratitude by adding a courtyard, a pylon (monumental gateway), colossal statues and obelisks to the Luxor temple.

Returning downstream, Ramesses II stopped at Abydos, a holy city and traditional burial place of Osiris, the god of resurrection. Ramesses later described in a dedicatory inscription what greeted him there: "He found the temples of the necropolis which belonged to former kings...fallen into a state of disrepair...no two bricks were together...No son was there who would refurbish the monument of his father." [1]

One of a number of colossal statues of King Ramesses II flanking the columns of the first court of the Luxor temple.

Instilled from an early age with a reverence for his ancestors, Ramesses II corrected the sad situation in Abydos by completing their temples, restoring their tombs and establishing their endowment in perpetuity. In a smart political move aimed at placing the priesthood firmly in his camp and under his control, he promoted a local Abydene priest, Nebwenenef, to the office of high priest of Amun at Thebes, the most powerful priestly position in the land.

Leaving Abydos, Ramesses continued north into Lower Egypt to the Eastern Delta near Avaris, probably the native city of his ancestors, where his father had erected a summer palace. It was in this area, close to the Waters of Ra (Pelusiac branch of the Nile), that Ramesses II decided to establish a new capital city. He named his city Pi-Ramesses (the House of Ramesses, beloved of Amun, Great of Victories), and he erected a heaven on earth.

Contemporary accounts hint at the magnificence of Pi-Ramesses. The king's palace, large and lavishly decorated, occupied a central location in the city. Its great limestone columns and its massive mudbrick walls, overlaid with a casing of glazed faience tiles, must have loomed high above the flatness of the Delta terrain. Doorways, window frames, balconies and the platform of the king's throne featured faience tile decorations showing foreign captives, vassals paying tribute and lions devouring prisoners, all calculated to awe the onlooker. The harem's decorative tiles, in contrast, featured lighthearted themes, such as floral designs (Cat. No. 39), aquatic life (Cat. Nos. 40-42) and carefree maidens (Cat. No. 43). These tiles, too, were made

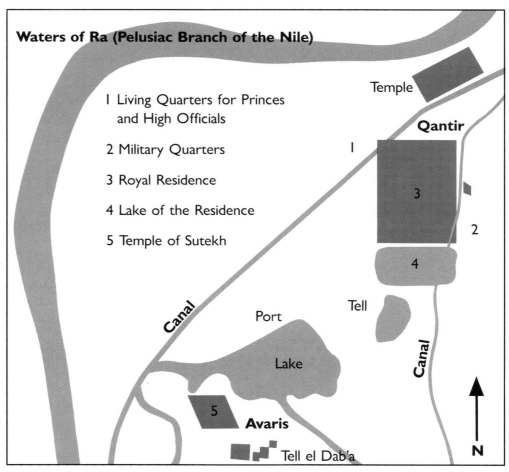

Pi-Ramesses in the Ramesside Age

Little remains of Ramesses II's Delta capital Pi-Ramesses, now under excavation by the Pelizaeus Museum, Hildesheim, West Germany.

One of at least 24 lofty obelisks erected by Ramesses the Great at Pi-Ramesses. Now they lie in ruin at Tanis.

Piece by piece, the temples, statues and obelisks of Pi-Ramesses were moved to the new capital at Tanis by the kings of Dynasty XXI.

from faience, a ceramic covered with glaze, and their color dazzled the eye. An official writing during the reign of Ramesses II's son, Merneptah, would liken the material to turquoise and lapis lazuli.

A large lake, living quarters for princes, priests and high-echelon bureaucrats, a military training ground and barracks, and a zoo occupied the area around the palace. (Lion, gazelle, giraffe and elephant bones aided archaeologists in identifying the site of the zoo.) Archives, administrative buildings, workshops, open-air markets, a harbor, warehouses and granaries, separated from each other by lakes and canals, also contributed to the bustling atmosphere of Pi-Ramesses.

The city continued to flourish after Ramesses II's reign, but slowly, over the next 200 years, the river branch which flowed to its west silted up and changed course northward. Pi-Ramesses was cut off, and the rulers of Dynasty XXI established a new capital city at Tanis. Rather than transport vast amounts of newly cut stone from distant quarries, they simply dismantled the monuments of Ramesses II's old capital and used the stone to build their own temples. Today, so little remains *in situ* from Ramesses II's grand Delta city that the average visitor to the original site, in the area of modern Qantir, would hardly be aware that an important ancient metropolis had ever existed there.

Ramesses II sponsored active building programs in other cities, especially Memphis, Egypt's first capital and her strongest link to the ancient past. We know less about Memphis than many other ancient capital cities because so much has been removed, destroyed by a rising water table or still lies buried. We do know, however, that the city grew and prospered under Ramesses II's rule. Of the extant monuments, the majority bear the cartouche of Ramesses the Great.

Memphis in the Ramesside Age was a political, military and religious hub. Central to the city, most likely, was the large temple precinct (ca. 3774 x 2625 feet) of Memphis' patron god, Ptah. Ramesses II may have been crowned here. According to a myth promoted by the Memphis priesthood, Ptah, in his role as creator of the universe, was the god of craftsmen, and workshops of many artisans were located outside his temple. Ramesses II's palace probably lay near the sacred area, but to date none of its remains have been identified.

With its location at the southern tip of the Delta, Memphis had truly been a "river city" from at least the time of the Old Kingdom. It guarded the entrance to the Nile Valley, and its harbor served as a departure point for ships destined for Mediterranean ports. (Because of silting, the river changed course, and the precise location of the Ramesside port awaits discovery.) Memphis was a vast ship-building center where seagoing vessels and boats of all sizes which traveled the Nile were constructed and repaired. The industry required timber yards, carpenters' workshops and toolmakers' quarters. Some of the ships produced in Memphis dockyards joined Pharaoh's fleet. The city's importance as a center of commerce and communication made it a strategic military area. Troops were garrisoned there, and infantry and chariotry conducted maneuvers and fought mock battles within the city's boundaries. Arsenals warehoused chariots and weapons which had been manufactured in Memphis workshops.

All the personnel required to staff and administer the military installations, workshops, palace, temples and port, as well as the auxiliary industries which grew up around them, made Memphis a key residential center, probably Egypt's largest.

The Ptah temple precinct at Memphis.

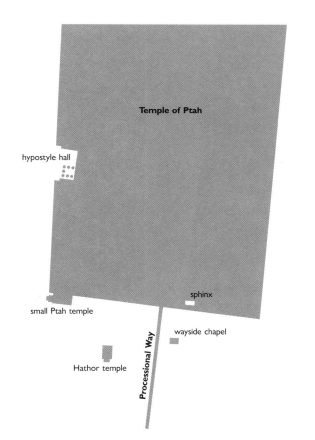

**Memphis in the Ramesside Age
Ptah Temple Precinct**

Temple of Ptah

hypostyle hall

small Ptah temple

sphinx

wayside chapel

Processional Way

Hathor temple

N

Houses and workshops of Ramesside artisans lie at the southwest corner of the Ptah temple precinct at Memphis. They were recently excavated by the Egypt Exploration Society.

A temple to Hathor in ancient
Memphis.

After a dreadful beating, enemy spies revealed the whereabouts of the Hittite troops. From Abu Simbel.

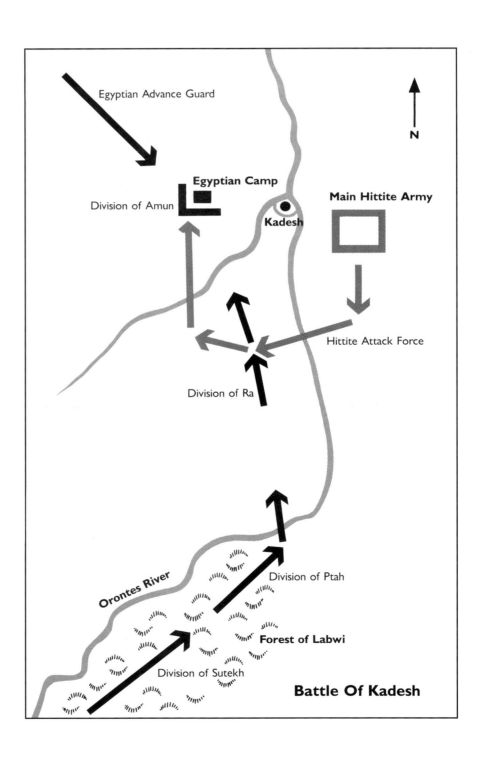

Egyptian Advance Guard

N

Egyptian Camp

Division of Amun

Kadesh

Main Hittite Army

Hittite Attack Force

Division of Ra

Orontes River

Division of Ptah

Forest of Labwi

Division of Sutekh

Battle Of Kadesh

A place of beauty and cultural vitality, Memphis enjoyed the devotion of her citizens. One homesick Memphite living at the end of Dynasty XIX wrote of how his heart "hastens to a place that it knows...Come to me, O Ptah, that you may take me to Memphis."[2] Another wrote, "The like of Memphis has never been seen."[3]

Warrior and Peacemaker

Rumors of trouble in the Levant in Year 4 forced Ramesses II to put aside his concentration upon the ongoing massive construction projects and focus his attention on less peaceful concerns. The relative stability of Egypt's vassal states along the eastern Mediterranean coast and her control of other vital trade routes of the Ancient Near East had been weakened since late in Dynasty XVIII by the growing strength of the Hittite empire in Anatolia (modern Turkey). As Prince-Regent, Ramesses II had accompanied his father on a campaign to the Levant to re-establish control of the coastal area and mastery over the city of Kadesh, an important crossroad in northern Amurru, an area that included Syria and Lebanon. Kadesh, straddling the northern tip of Lebanon's mountain ranges and controlling passage south into the Bekaa Valley and east from there through the Eleutheros Valley to the sea, had again fallen under Hittite control. Ramesses II was determined to recapture the prize.

In April of Year 5, Ramesses the Great left Egypt with an army of about 20,000 men, one of the largest military forces the Near East had ever seen. Four divisions of about 5,000 men each made the long march north along the coast of Canaan, then inland to the Bekaa Valley. Meanwhile, Pharaoh's advance guard, a small force of the king's elite, moved forward along a different route. Each division included infantry and chariotry; each traveled under the divine protection and standard of one of Egypt's main gods and under the command of Ramesses II or one of his sons. The entire force, with its chariots, herald trumpeters, supply wagons and camp followers, must have stretched for miles. This army, traveling an estimated two miles per hour, might have covered 15 miles on a good day.

Within a month the Egyptian forces reached the Orontes River, less than ten miles from Kadesh. A pair of captured spies lied, asserting that the enemy forces were still some 120 miles to the north near Aleppo. Therefore, Ramesses II's Amun division, followed closely by the Ra Division, crossed the Orontes and continued toward Kadesh, establishing camp just west of the city. Then Egyptian scouts seized two more spies who, after a hearty flogging, begged for mercy and revealed that the Hittite

King Ramesses II repulses the Hittites. From Luxor.

army was actually only minutes away on the other side of Kadesh! Upon hearing this dreadful news, Ramesses II immediately dispatched mounted messengers to summon his troops, half of which had yet to ford the Orontes. Moments later, the Hittites attacked.

Under the Hittite banner, King Muwatallis had amassed an army even larger than Egypt's. Hired mercenaries and pirates from a vast area had joined native Hittites to make up two groups of fighting men about 18,000 and 19,000 strong. In addition, there were 2,500 chariots. The Hittite chariotry now smashed into the division of Ra which was behind that of Amun. In frenzied flight from charging chariots, the soldiers of Ra burst into Ramesses II's encamped Amun Division, which also scattered in panic.

Finding himself abandoned by all but his personal guard and his shield-bearer, Ramesses II prayed to the god Amun: "I call upon thee, my father Amun, for I am in the midst of a multitude of foes."[4] And Amun gave him strength. Virtually alone, Ramesses II charged the enemy in his chariot. "All about him was the heat of fire,"[5] according to one inscription. "He was mighty, his heart stout."[6]

Fortunately, just at that moment, Ramesses II's elite advance guard, which had been traveling a separate route to Kadesh, appeared and entered the battle. Attacked now from two flanks, the Hittites hastily retreated. King Muwatallis sent auxiliaries, but to no avail. A third Egyptian force, the division of Ptah, had arrived and joined the melee. When Ramesses II set up camp that night on the battlefield, even the cowardly warriors from Amun and Ra came drifting back. The next day Ramesses led them in a fresh onslaught. The battle ended in a stalemate.

For the Hittites, it had been a near disaster. With the bulk of his chariotry captured, a brother killed and many of his chief officers wounded, King Muwatallis begged for peace.

It must have been a joyous moment in camp, as the Egyptian forces surveyed their booty of chariots, horses, armor, bows, arrows, swords, daggers, shields and prisoners. To calculate enemy casualties, Egyptian soldiers lopped off the hands of the dead Hittite soldiers, tossing them in a pile as scribes recorded their numbers.

Ramesses II led his troops home in triumph and proclaimed to the four corners of the earth how his heroism in the face of adversity had saved the day. The story of the Battle of Kadesh is related in prose, poetry and illustration on temples he built throughout the land. It can be seen today at Abydos, Karnak, twice at the Ramesseum (his funerary temple near the Valley of the Kings) and three times at Luxor. In Nubia it may be seen at Abu Simbel, and it once existed at Derr as well. Each time Ramesses II told the story, it became a bit more elaborate, but in every case he

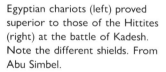

Egyptian chariots (left) proved superior to those of the Hittites (right) at the battle of Kadesh. Note the different shields. From Abu Simbel.

Ramesses II slays foreign enemies. From Memphis.

neglected to point out that, despite his valor, the battle had changed nothing. The Hittites, after all, retained possession of Kadesh.

For a full 15 years following the Battle of Kadesh, skirmishes and constantly shifting alliances continued to plague the Egyptian empire at its borders. Those years saw Ramesses II back on the battlefield in Canaan, Lebanon and Syria, as petty kingdoms resisted Egyptian supremacy and neglected to send tribute.

Then, following the death of old King Muwatallis who had fought at Kadesh, the situation changed. His brother, after deposing and banishing a nephew, assumed power as King Hattusil III. Because of his relatively insecure position internally and the Assyrian empire's growing strength to his east, Hattusil III could ill afford another military debacle with his country's old enemy, Egypt. Instead, Ramesses II tells us, the new Hittite king sent messengers to Egypt to propose a formal peace treaty. (According to Hattusil III, Ramesses II approached the Hittites!)

How long it took for the two great powers to agree on terms we do not know. However, in November or December of 1259 B.C., Year 21 of Ramesses II's rule, three Hittite ambassadors arrived in Pi-Ramesses bearing two silver tablets inscribed in Akkadian cuneiform, the *lingua franca* of the day, with terms mutually agreed upon. At approximately the same time, three Egyptian officials arrived in Hattusas, the Hittite capital, with two similar tablets.

This remarkable treaty survives today in the Hittite version on two clay tablets found in a temple in the Hittite capital and in the Egyptian version carved on temple walls at Karnak and at the Ramesseum. Although it is neither the earliest ancient treaty, nor wholly original in its content, it is the sole treaty for which versions from both parties survive. Clearly, it demonstrates that, in addition to being a brave warrior, Ramesses II was an effective statesman. The issues the treaty dealt with are as timely today as they were when he was in power:

> *Mutual nonaggression:* Each side desired peace, and each agreed not to attack the other. (Boundaries, however, were not mentioned.)
>
> *Mutual defense:* If a third party should attack, each would aid the other.
>
> *Rightful succession of heirs.*
>
> *Mutual extradition of fugitives:* They were to be guaranteed humane treatment.
>
> *Witnesses:* One thousand gods of Egypt and 1000 gods of Hatti blessed the treaty. Curses would befall anybody who broke its terms!

Soon after the treaty was negotiated, letters of greeting and good wishes were exchanged between the royal families. King wrote to king, and queen to queen, adding a uniquely personal note to ancient international diplomacy. Envoys also carried greetings to the Hittite king from Queen Mother Tuya, Crown Prince Amunherkhopeshef and Vizier of the South, Paser. Gifts of jewelry and clothing were exchanged as well. On one occasion, when Hattusil III expressed his displeasure at what he interpreted as an arrogant tone, Ramesses II quickly responded with a denial and an apology accompanied by rich presents, including medicinal herbs and a skilled physician to administer them. We are aware of this wonderful demonstration of international pique and etiquette thanks to excavations in the temples and archives of the Hittite capital.

Two thousand gods had borne witness that evil would befall anyone who broke the treaty's terms. As far as we know, no one did. It appears that Ramesses II had laid down his arms for good by this time and returned to his building projects. Even 50 years later, his son and successor, Merneptah, would record on the walls of Karnak that he came to the aid of his brothers, the Hittites, by shipping them grain when famine ravaged their land.

Tia and Tia, sister and brother-in-law of Ramesses II, were buried together at Saqqara. Remains of their pyramid are in the foreground. Their tomb was recently discovered by the joint Egypt Exploration Society-Rijksmuseum van Oudheden.

The Royal Family

Ramesses II was very much a family man, perhaps more so than any other king whose records remain. His devotion to his mother, Tuya (Cat. No. 3), is clear from the number of monuments he erected in her honor. Ramesses II had at least two brothers and two sisters, one of whom, Tia, served as divine chantress in Memphis, Heliopolis and Pi-Ramesses. Her husband, also named Tia, was appointed by Ramesses II to the office of Superintendent both of the Treasury and of the Cattle of the Ramesseum.

Among his wives, Ramesses' favorite was clearly the beautiful Nefertari, who bore the titles Great Royal Wife and Mistress of Upper and Lower Egypt. Ramesses dedicated a temple to her, as the ideal woman and mother. Like only a few previous Egyptian queens, Nefertari enjoyed a political role, appearing beside her husband on state occasions and participating in the Hittite diplomatic exchanges. She was the mother of the king's first-born son, Crown Prince Amunherkhopeshef, and before Queen Nefertari passed on to the netherworld during Ramesses II's third decade of rule, she bore at least three additional sons and two daughters. Her tomb is the most beautifully decorated sepulcher in the Valley of the Queens in Western Thebes. An inscription on its walls names Nefertari ''Possessor of charm, sweetness and love.'' Her veneration continued even after her death.

Although first in the king's affections, Queen Nefertari was not his sole royal consort. A lesser queen named Istnofret was mother to his second son (Ramesses), his fourth (Khaemwase) and his thirteenth (Merneptah), as well as to his first daughter. Elevated to the position of chief wife upon Nefertari's death, Istnofret lived until approximately Year 34 of Ramesses II's rule. Meanwhile, the king's sister, Henutmire, and his daughters, Meryetamun (Cat. No. 4), Bint-Anath and Nebettawy, also received the title Great Royal Wife.

A Hittite princess, King Hattusil III's daughter to whom the Egyptians gave the name Maathorneferure, became one of Ramesses II's chief wives in Year 34. Diplomatic "state" marriages were not uncommon in Ancient Near Eastern society, for both sides profited. To renew their bonds of friendship and to reconfirm their peace treaty of Year 21, King Hattusil III, some 13 years later, offered his oldest daughter to Ramesses II in marriage (or so states the Egyptian account). Her lavish dowry undoubtedly made this offer especially attractive to Ramesses II.

In late fall of 1246 B.C., the Hittite princess left her homeland accompanied by

Of his many wives, Nefertari was Ramesses II's favorite, based upon the many monuments he built in her honor. Her tomb at Thebes contains some of the finest painting of the Ramesside era.

ambassadors, dignitaries and soldiers who guarded not only this retinue but also, according to one of the commemorative stelae later erected, "a very great tribute...of gold, silver, copper in great quantities, slaves, horses without limit, cattle, goats and sheep by the ten-thousands." [7] Ramesses II sent his delegation to meet the Hittites and regally escort them to Egypt. On a delightfully balmy February day in 1245 B.C. (weather arranged courtesy of Pharaoh through a special prayer to Sutekh in his role as god of the weather), the party arrived at the gates at Pi-Ramesses. There Ramesses II gazed for the first time upon his bride, and, we are told, "She was beautiful in the heart of his majesty, and he loved her more than anything." [8]

So proud was he of his new bride that he proclaimed her arrival throughout the land. The text of the "Marriage Stela" has been found at Karnak, on the isle of Elephantine at Aswan, and further south in Nubia at Aksha, Abu Simbel and Amara West. In later state marriages, Ramesses II took another Hittite princess, a Babylonian princess and a Syrian princess into his harem.

Exactly how many children Ramesses II's great royal wives and his lesser wives bore, we do not know, but recent assessments place the number at around 90 (approximately 50 boys and 40 girls). Sons and daughters appear with the king in birth-order procession on temple walls and beside him on statuary. Sons accompanied him in battle. Like his father before him, Ramesses II trained them in the art of kingship.

As adults, some of Ramesses the Great's children aided him in administering the country and promoting his ideals. His fourth son, Khaemwase, inherited his father's interest in Egypt's splendid past and became the country's first archaeologist. He was later revered by Greek and Roman conquerors of Egypt as a scholar and a magician. Appointed to the priesthood at Memphis as a youth and eventually assuming the office of high priest, Khaemwase studied the ancient writings and, by the time of his death in Year 55 of his father's reign, he had systematically restored the Old Kingdom pyramids at Giza and Saqqara which, even then, were more than a thousand years old.

Khaemwase, dressed as a high priest, kneels beside an image of Memphis' god, Ptah-Tatenen. From Memphis.

Ramesses II erected a stela chapel (right) at Gebel Silsileh in honor of Hapi, god of the Nile flood. Sety I's virtually identical monument may be seen to the left.

As part of the celebration of his jubilee festival, Ramesses II ran around a course four times to symbolize his taking possession of the land. From Beit el Wali.

The King Divine and Eternal

In Ramesses the Great's Egypt, as decade followed decade, peace and prosperity prevailed. Ramesses II was increasingly concerned with establishing himself as a god in the eyes of his people and ensuring that he would live and rule forever.

Through the traditional jubilee festival *(hebsed)*, beginning in Year 30, he sought to renew his youthfulness and power. The jubilee was celebrated (in theory, at least) only after a king had occupied the throne for 30 years. It was then repeated approximately every three years thereafter. The jubilee reinvigorated the aging monarch, reaffirmed his right to rule and re-enacted his coronation. For the subjects of Ramesses the Great, it was a new experience, since almost 100 years had passed since a traditional jubilee was last celebrated (in the long reign of Amunhotep III). Ramesses II would eventually celebrate 14 jubilees, more than any other king in Egypt's history.

For several months before his first jubilee festival in 1249 B.C., the king's son, Khaemwase, in his role as high priest of Memphis, must have traveled the land proclaiming the great event. Records of his announcement, in the form of stelae and inscriptions, are found particularly in Egypt's southern border areas, namely, Aswan, where it was believed the Nile floods began, and Gebel Silsileh, an area sacred to Hapi, god of the Nile flood. In a sense, the jubilee was similar to a flood, for just as the Nile's deposit of fertile silt rejuvenated the land, so too did his jubilee festival rejuvenate the king. In fact, Ramesses the Great boasted later that the Nile flood rose especially high at that time. (Supporting evidence, however, is lacking.)

Exactly where the king celebrated his jubilees is unclear. Whether the first was in Memphis or perhaps at Pi-Ramesses, large crowds must have gathered to witness the event. When the time arrived, the thirtieth anniversary of the king's accession, a procession formed. Ramesses the Great, dressed in a knee-length cloak and followed by priests and high officials, entered a special temple precinct. There, he gave gifts to the gods, and they responded by granting him hundreds of thousands of years of rule and by renewing *Ma'at*, society's divine order. To demonstrate his triumph and renewal and to symbolize his taking possession of the land, the king then sprinted around a special track. This was followed by singing, dancing, feasting and all manner of joyous celebration.

After his second jubilee festival, Ramesses II made another addition to his name, explaining that he was "Lord of Jubilees, like his father Ptah-Tatenen." Not only did Ramesses II associate himself with Egypt's gods, but he had now become one of them in his own eyes. In Nubia, especially, where he enjoyed greatest independence from Egypt's priesthood, his deification was proclaimed repeatedly.

In his later years the king spent much of his time at Pi-Ramesses. From there he saw Egypt's cities grow, her temples thrive and her people prosper. His peace with the Hittites continued, despite great changes in the Ancient Near East, and the world paid him homage. As jubilee followed jubilee, the divine promise of hundreds of thousands of years appeared to be coming true. Ramesses II would outlive not only many of his wives, but also his first 12 sons!

II
Egypt in the Ramesside Age

Gods of the Nile flood hold Egypt's
riches at the temple of Ramesses II
at Abydos.

The goddess Isis suckles the young Ramesses II. From Beit el Wali.

Ramesses II pays homage to his own image included (second from right) among the gods at Wadi Sebua.

Villagers worshiped awesome images of Ramesses the Great. From Luxor.

As visitors to today's Egypt soon realize, Ramesses II's huge stone buildings still mark the landscape at almost every ancient site. Temples he erected, statuary he commissioned, monuments he inscribed and the funerary temple and royal tomb he built for himself all provide first-hand information about his life and his world, as he wished posterity to know them. However, the fascination that Egyptian civilization holds for us stems not just from the splendor of monuments and the glory of kings. It comes also from evidence that our ancient counterparts grappled with moral, ethical and practical concerns similar to ours and evolved explanations and solutions that have, in many cases, maintained their validity over the millennia.

Such evidence is found in the mudbrick remains of the cities Ramesses II built—palaces, public buildings, workshops, the houses of citizens and the remains of their material possessions. It also still exists in copious archival records on papyrus (ancient paper made from the stem of the plant flattened and pressed together, as Cat. No. 57) and on scraps of inscribed limestone or pottery known as ostraca (Cat. Nos. 12 and 56). These reveal the minutiae of everyday life—prices and wages, lawsuits, marriages and divorces, farm production, taxes, labor problems. Such information reflects the people's hopes and fears and their relation to their gods.

Worship of the Gods

Ramesses II lived in a divine land. Happiness on earth and eternal life in the netherworld, for king and commoner alike, depended directly upon the care and attention lavished on the myriad gods who oversaw Egypt's proper functioning. On a cosmic sphere, different gods represented and controlled the sun, moon, sky, earth, air and Nile flood. Each city also had its own local god or gods responsible for the well-being of its citizenry and often credited with its creation. When cities gained particular prominence politically, as Pi-Ramesses, Memphis and Thebes did in Ramesses II's Egypt, their local gods grew in prestige and power. Average villagers had little access to these awesome state gods, so on a daily basis, they worshiped more intimate, more approachable gods who saw specifically to their needs.

The king presented still another avenue for prayer and personal worship. The office of kingship was divine. Ramesses II, like every other Egyptian king, was the product of the union between a heavenly father and an earthly mother. Goddesses suckled him and supervised his upbringing. Certain named statues of him represented Ramesses II's kingly office deified, and they, too, were regarded as divine. The colossal statues of him that stood in pairs outside temples throughout the land acted as intermediaries between passers-by and the great gods at home inside. Pious villagers and high officials alike might offer a petition or erect a stela to the cult of the king. In this manner, Ramesses the Great, deified, was benefactor to all. (On occasion, Ramesses II, the mortal, is himself shown worshiping a statue of Ramesses II, the god!)

What the gods had created, the king inherited. Ramesses II's duty was to preserve the union of Upper and Lower Egypt which was secured in his name. He did this by defeating Egypt's enemies, defined as the forces of chaos, and by honoring the gods. In almost every ancient city, Ramesses II built new temples to the local deities or added to existing ones.

Egyptian temples, as homes of the gods, replicated the legendary structure of the universe at the time of creation. A mudbrick enclosure wall separated the sacred area inside—the primeval hill which rose from a watery chaos at the beginning of time,

Originally, six statues and two obelisks flanked Ramesses the Great's entrance to the temple of Luxor. In the last century one of the obelisks was moved to the Place de la Concorde in Paris.

The gods Horus and Thoth tie the plants of Upper and Lower Egypt around windpipe and lungs, the hieroglyph meaning "unite." Above, Ramesses II clutches the crook of kingship.

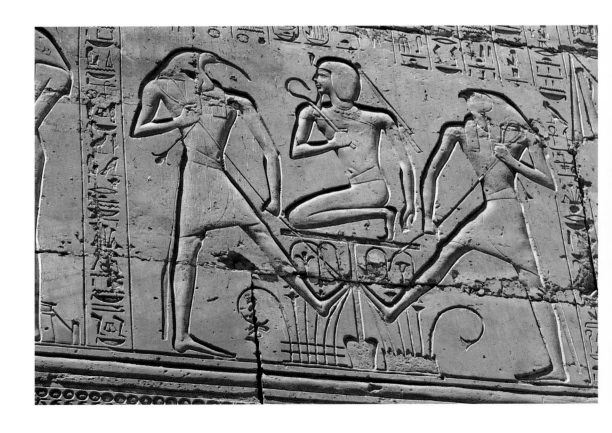

according to one creation myth—from the profane world outside. Soaring obelisks, colossal statues, fierce sphinxes and brightly colored flags flanked the temple entrance. A monumental gateway, or pylon, led to a large open-air court where crowds might gather for festivals. On the court's far side, a doorway led to a somewhat smaller area, a room filled with rows of columns and known as a hypostyle hall. Floral capitals on the columns and often a papyrus and swamp motif at the bottom of the walls enclosing the hall reproduced the marshy landscape and luxuriant plant life at the beginning of the world. Rays of sunlight, filtering down between the many columns from the tiny windows high above, created a shadowy, other-worldly effect inside, in contrast to the brightness of the open-air court.

The hypostyle hall served as a passageway into the temple's tiny, dimly lit, innermost chamber, its focal point. Here, in this holy of holies, under a star-decorated ceiling (the vault of heaven), the image of the god resided. Access to this sacred place was permitted only to the highest priests whose duty it was to see that the gods were cared for, nourished and entertained.

In theory, the king was the high priest of every temple, but in practice, others usually took his place. Every morning as the sun rose, the chief priests, purified after bathing in the god's sacred lake, entered the temple chanting and burning incense. They carefully broke the seals, slid the lock's heavy bolt then swung open the doors of the inner sanctuary. Bowing and singing, they stepped inside and greeted the god. They washed and anointed him with precious unguents, dressed him in fine linen and adorned him with jewels. More prayers, singing and incense accompanied his morning meal. With reverent bows, they then resealed his door until the next rituals. Lesser priests maintained the temple and cared for minor gods.

More elaborate ceremonies marked such festivals as the Beautiful Feast of the Valley (Cat. No. 11), or the Opet Festival, when the god's statue, carefully shrouded from public view, was placed on its sacred barque and carried on the shoulders of priests through the hypostyle hall to the waiting throngs outside. Only at such times was the great god directly accessible to all for petition or prayer.

Some gods received special attention by virtue of the political power of the city from which they came, their connection to the king's family origins, their universal role or their previous importance. When he built Pi-Ramesses, his opulent capital city in the Delta, Ramesses II marked its four cardinal points with temples to four different gods.

To the west lay the Amun temple. Because Amun was a major god of the New Kingdom monarchy, his temples were found in every major Egyptian city. To the south lay the sacred precinct of Sutekh (later called Seth), the god for whom Ramesses II's father, Sety I, had been named. Sutekh was associated with the Hyksos, invaders from the East who ruled Egypt from Avaris, where Ramesside family roots appear to lie. Sutekh also represented turbulence and unrestrained power, and when he later fell out of favor at the end of the New Kingdom, his name came to signify evil. Marking Pi-Ramesses' eastern side was a temple to another deity of Asiatic origin, Astarte, a goddess of both war and love. New Kingdom Egyptians, associating her with their maternal goddesses Hathor and Isis, assimilated Astarte into the Egyptian pantheon. To the north was a temple to Wadjet, the cobra goddess and titulary deity of Lower Egypt. In her form as a uraeus or snake, Wadjet entwined herself around the brow of the king to protect him and destroy his enemies with her fiery venom. Although literature provides most of our information about Pi-Ramesses' temples since so little actually remains, there is archaeological evidence that the king

Kneeling, Ramesses the Great presents a table filled with food offerings and a jar of a liquid libation to the gods.

Sutekh, represented as a hybrid animal with a long snout, protects an image of the king.

A villager kneels beside the toes of a colossal statue of Ramesses II from Pi-Ramesses. Originally the statue stood almost 33 feet high!

A stela dedicated to both Egyptian and Syrian deities bears testimony to the cosmopolitan religious climate of the Egypt of Ramesses the Great.

also built temples there to honor, among others, Ptah, god of Memphis, and Ra-Horakhty, a solar deity and primeval creator god whose homeland was Heliopolis.

The number of lesser known Egyptian gods, composite gods and gods of foreign origin venerated in Pi-Ramesses testifies to that city's liberal religious climate and the magnitude of its religious establishment. Needless to say, the cult of the king, represented by colossal statues of Ramesses II, figured prominently and formed a focus of worship for the average citizen. Although only fragments of the actual colossi from Pi-Ramesses remain, the existence of more than 60 votive stelae from the site, which depict their owners worshiping a named statue of Ramesses II, provides evidence of their one-time importance.

In Ramesside Memphis, the precinct of the temple of Ptah was the only rival in size to the precinct of Amun at Karnak. Ptah, because of Memphis' importance, had gained a universal following. He was the patron of artists and craftsmen, because, as a creator god, he had conceived the world in his heart and had brought it into being by speaking aloud its qualities and agencies. Like many other city gods, he was part of a divine family consisting of his consort, Sakhmet, and their son, Nefertum. Ramesses the Great often associated Ptah with Tatenen, another earth god of Memphis, and he worshiped the composite Ptah-Tatenen. So proud was Ramesses II of his expansion of Ptah's Memphis temple that in Year 35 of his reign he boasted about it in the so-called "Blessings of Ptah" inscription found at Abu Simbel, almost 800 miles to the south. He added a hall to the western side of the temple, perhaps erected in honor of one of his jubilees, and he may have rebuilt parts of the Ptah temple's main structure, using "stone, covered in gold and precious stones."[9] Colossal statues of the king stood outside the temple's gateways or in front of wayside shrines which formed a processional way leading to the main south gate. To date, 11 complete or fragmentary colossi

The army trumpeter, Hesi, worships a colossus of Ramesses II named "User-Ma'at-Ra Setep-en-Ra (throne name of Ramesses II) Montu in the Two Lands."

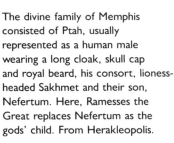

The divine family of Memphis consisted of Ptah, usually represented as a human male wearing a long cloak, skull cap and royal beard, his consort, lioness-headed Sakhmet and their son, Nefertum. Here, Ramesses the Great replaces Nefertum as the gods' child. From Herakleopolis.

have been found at Memphis. Also, two smaller Memphis temples, which Ramesses II may have erected in celebration of his first or second jubilee, lay west and south of the main temple precinct—one to Ptah, complete with pylon, gateway and triple shrines, and another to Hathor. Once quite splendid, they are still picturesque in their ruined state.

At Thebes, a major religious center of Egypt's empire, Ramesses built lavishly, especially at Karnak, the splendid temple home of the Theban patron god Amun. This god's name meant "Hidden One," and his "family" consisted of a consort, Mut, and their son, Khonsu. King of the gods and father of kings, Amun, like Ptah, was credited with the creation of the world. Generally represented as a human male, Amun also took the form of a ram (Cat. No. 12) or a gander.

The Amun precinct at Karnak now fills approximately 60 acres, but it had not yet reached that extent when Ramesses the Great built a landing dock on the west side toward the Nile and connected it to the temple entrance with an avenue of 120 ram-headed sphinxes, which sheltered the king's image. Inside, Ramesses completed the decoration of Karnak's lofty, columned hypostyle hall and ordered that it be open for public worship (of himself particularly). He called it "The Place Where the Common People Extol the Name of His Majesty."

This hall, begun by Ramesses II's grandfather and partially decorated by his father, Sety I, contained 134 columns with a papyrus motif. On an outside wall of the hall, Ramesses II had carved scenes of his wars in Canaan and Syria and incorporated a

Ramesses II built a small temple to Ptah in Memphis just south of the god's main temple.

A lone Hathor-head capital from the Ptah temple precinct at Memphis.

Ramesses II, wearing divine headgear, sits with arms entwined between Amun and his consort, Mut, patron deities of Thebes. Usually they are represented with their son, Khonsu. From Thebes.

copy of his peace treaty with the Hittites. He covered an inside wall with sacred scenes that included his divine coronation, and he partially usurped the reliefs commissioned by his father, Sety I, which covered another wall. Dynasty XIX Thebans undoubtedly were awestruck upon entering this forest of towering columns which let in only enough light to illuminate the images of Ramesses II (and Sety I) among the gods. As a further display of his own grandeur and omnipotence, Ramesses II also sponsored a gateway on Karnak's east side and erected two colossi of himself in the form of Osiris, god of resurrection, flanking the entry of a Dynasty XVIII shrine.

About two miles south of Karnak lay the temple of Luxor, built largely by Amunhotep III of Dynasty XVIII and visited each year during the Opet Festival by Amun's cult image from the Karnak temple. (It was at Luxor that Ramesses II had honored Amun by adding a colonnaded court, pylon, obelisks and colossi—of himself—after personally officiating as high priest at the Opet Festival in the first year of his rule.)

The ram of Amun protects an image
of Ramesses II. From Karnak.

Ramesses II erected an avenue of
ram-headed sphinxes leading to the
temple of Karnak.

At the "Temple of Ramesses, Beloved of Amun, Hearer of Prayer" at Karnak's east gate, passers-by prayed to statues of the king so that he might speak on their behalf to the gods at home inside.

134 columns arranged in 16 rows
form the hypostyle hall at Karnak.
This architectural masterwork, the
largest hall of columns in the world,
occupies an area of 53,800 square
feet.

Wadi Sebua at its original site in Nubia. The temple is dedicated to Amun, Ra-Horakhty and Ramesses II.

Sphinxes at Wadi Sebua in Nubia bear the head of Ramesses the Great wearing the double crown. "Sebua" is Arabic for lion.

In Egypt proper—that is, the Delta and Nile Valley (to Aswan)—Ramesses II's self-glorifying activities and the image he presented were governed by tradition and were held in check by powerful temple clergy. However, in far-off Nubia, the 800-mile stretch of land south of Aswan, no such constraints applied. No major Nubian town or strategically significant area was left untouched as Ramesses II built anew or embellished over a dozen temples. In Nubia, especially in the many temples completed after his second jubilee, Ramesses the Great became a resident deity.

Many of Ramesses II's Nubian temples are familiar to us because of international efforts, during the building of the Aswan High Dam in the 1960s, to record and or move them to higher ground before they were covered by rising waters. The list includes Beit el Wali, Gerf Hussein, Wadi Sebua, Derr, Abu Simbel, Amara West and Aksha. These southern temples replicated most elements of sanctuaries throughout Egypt proper, and they typically incorporated hard sandstone from the Nubian cliffs as part of their matrix. Often the hypostyle hall was cut into the face of the cliff, and the holy of holies, the shrine housing cult statues of the temple's resident gods, was carved deeper still into the mountain. The Nubian temples were exceptional in the integration of colossal royal images into their architecture. Sphinxes bearing Ramesses the Great's features guarded the entryways; statues of him *en masse* served as pillars; and he resided among other gods as their equal in the holy of holies. Made by local artisans, these statues often replaced in volume what they lacked in sophistication.

Perhaps the most famous of Ramesses II's Nubian projects—the two temples on the Nile's west bank that are cut deep into the sandstone cliffs at Abu Simbel—is also his greatest achievement. These temples now lie 215 feet higher than they did when Ramesses II first commissioned the work, probably sometime after his fifth regnal year. His original purpose was to honor Egypt's major gods and their local Nubian variants. However, as the impressive images of himself were carved on the facade and pillars of the first temple and its walls were covered with a record of his military exploits, Ramesses the Great's ideas about who he was began to change. He ordered artisans to re-carve scenes of the gods at the back of the first hall to include himself. From the second hall back, he receives prominence equal to that of his fellow gods. In the end, the main temple at Abu Simbel, completed sometime after the king's 35th regnal year, became a temple to Ramesses the Great. He called it "The House of Ramesses, Beloved of Amun."

The image of the goddess Mut was moved to the right so a representation of Ramesses II might be added to a row of gods. From Abu Simbel.

Osiride pillars in the hypostyle hall leading to the sanctuary at Abu Simbel.

Opposite page. Ramesses the Great with his family at his feet from his temple at Abu Simbel.

The temples of Abu Simbel at their
new site above the waters of Lake
Nasser.

Ramesses the Great built a temple in honor of his favorite wife, the beautiful Nefertari. She died before it was finished.

The god Ra-Horakhty clasps
the *User* sign in his right hand
and a *Ma'at* sign in his left. Together
the composition may be read
User-Ma'at-Ra, the throne name
of Ramesses II.

The quarries at Gebel Silsileh provided sandstone for building projects from pharaonic times until the twentieth century A.D.

Perhaps a flaw in the stone caused quarrymen to abandon this colossal statue in the Aswan granite quarries.

Comparatively little is known about the many quarrying expeditions which took place during Ramesses II's rule. We may assume, however, that they were similar to a later expedition that set forth under royal auspices during the reign of Ramesses IV (1154-1148 B.C.), when High Priest of Amun Ramesses-nakht (Cat. No 27) led a granite-quarrying gang of 8,362 men and overseers to Wadi Hammamat in the Eastern Desert. Such quarry missions required the efforts of skilled specialists, untrained laborers, stone movers, tool sharpeners, baggage handlers, provision suppliers and errand runners. Quarry sites must have looked like small towns, equipped with temples, administrative buildings, processing areas and huts for workers whose job it was to turn mountains into building blocks cut to exact specifications for each project.

Quarrying methods were well-defined. Copper chisels, wooden mallets and heavy stone balls were used to pound out trenches in the rock around all four sides of the desired area and to drive wooden wedges beneath it. When moistened, the wedges expanded and helped to detach the block from the stone below. Finer finishing was done by skilled personnel using more delicate chisels, adzes, mallets and rubbing stones, aided by cubit rods (Cat. No. 30), right angles (Cat. No. 31) and plumb lines (Cat. No. 32). Ships and barges then transported the blocks to workshops and building sites where artisans and architects enjoyed working conditions decidedly more comfortable than those at the quarry! There the intense rays of the sun bouncing off

According to Ramesses II, he rewarded his quarrymen with all manner of succulent foods.

desert cliffs often sent temperatures soaring above 140° Fahrenheit, making the quarryman's life all but intolerable for a good part of the year. Hard manual labor under such conditions clearly caused high fatality rates. Ramesses IV's expedition to Wadi Hammamat lost over 900 men!

Still, Ramesses II would like us to believe that he treated his workmen well and that "their hearts were happy, their arms strong." [17] His quarrymen, he relates, were provided with clothing, sandals and ointment. They received excellent care, ample reward and feasted on cakes, wine, bread, barley, fish and beans. (Sagely he comments that workers perform best "when the belly is satisfied." [18]) Despite the king's humanitarian claims, it must be concluded that his myriad building projects, by their very number and size, involved the exploitation of many laborers. Some of the

Forty overseers were each required to deliver 2,000 bricks according to the inscription on a roll of leather written in Ramesses II's fifth regnal year.

workers were clearly foreign captives or prisoners forced to serve their terms doing hard labor.

Among them, in all probability, were a group of Near Easterners, the Hebrews who, according to the Bible, fled servitude in the land of Goshen (Egypt's fertile Eastern Delta region). As related in the Book of Exodus, the Hebrews, led by Moses, escaped from Egypt by crossing the Red Sea (probably the Reed Sea, a marshy area near the Sinai border). Pharaoh's pursuing charioteers, intent on preventing the flight of so many skilled laborers, were drowned in their attempt to follow them through the water. The Bible also tells us that Moses and his followers then wandered for 40 years in the Sinai desert, overcoming hardship after hardship, before finally making their way to a new homeland in the land of Canaan on the shores of the Eastern Mediterranean.

The Egyptians in their writings make no mention of this event, but in view of the propagandistic nature of ancient Egyptian official histories (including, of course, those of Ramesses II), this omission of the Exodus is understandable. What became a central event in the history of the nation of Israel was probably only a minor annoyance to mighty Egypt. Indeed, in ancient Egyptian records, the people of Israel are mentioned only once, on a stela inscribed in Year 5 of the reign of Ramesses II's son and successor, Merneptah. Erected in commemoration of a victory over the Libyans, the so-called ''Israel Stela'' also lists all the cities and tribes in Syria and Canaan that Merneptah had similarly defeated. The fact that Israel is so listed provides clear (and significant) evidence that by the fifth year after the death of Ramesses II, the desert wanderings of the people of Israel had ended. Assuming 40 years for these wanderings, if the Exodus took place at least 40 years prior to the Israel Stela and no more than 71 (66 years of Ramesses II's rule plus five years of Merneptah's), then the departure from Egypt would have occurred during Ramesses the Great's regency. Accordingly, Ramesses the Great and Moses may have been contemporaries.

Egypt's bustling cities and splendid temples made her prosperity visible. Since silver, copper and gold were mediums of exchange, the weight and amount of her precious metal resources made Egypt's wealth quantifiable. (Coinage was not yet in use and would not exist in Egypt until the end of Pharaonic times in the fourth century B.C.)

Prior to the New Kingdom, silver's rarity had made it highly prized, but in Ramesses II's day it arrived in such quantity as tribute from Asia, Crete and Libya that it was only half as valuable as gold. The value of copper was about 1/100th that of silver during Ramesses II's rule, and it came chiefly from Sinai, Syria and Cyprus. Copper's abundance and the ease with which it could be mined led to its wide use in everything from weaponry to cooking pots.

Glistening, corrosion-proof and malleable, gold was the most precious metal. Its value far transcended its exchange rate. Because it brought to mind the imperishable sun and its radiant life-giving qualities, gold was identified with the gods, and gold mining was a privilege reserved for kings and for temples. Most gold entered Egypt from Nubia as tribute. Although we lack production figures, we know the mines of Wawat, in Lower Nubia between the Nile's First and Second Cataracts, and those of Kush, farther upriver between the Second and Fourth Cataracts, were among the most productive. The Wadi Hammamat mines in Egypt proper also yielded gold.

On the ''Israel Stela,'' King Merneptah lists Israel among Egypt's conquered peoples.

The world's earliest map shows the location of the gold mines of Wadi Hammamat.

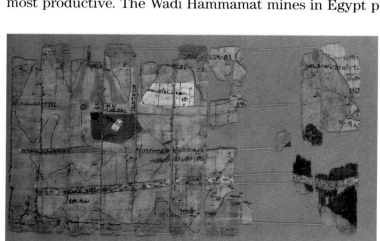

The Biblical Land of Goshen refers to the fertile Eastern Delta regions.

The Sinai desert at Mount Sinai.

Gold mining, like stone quarrying, was a difficult task. Gold mining gangs probably resembled quarry gangs, consisting mostly of prisoners of war, criminals and soldiers, as well as policemen who made sure they did not escape. Gold lay both in veins within the quartz rock and in alluvial gravels washed into long dry river beds or *wadis*. To separate metal from stone, the rocks and gravels had to be excavated with heavy tools, crushed into powder and then washed.

One of the main problems confronting a gold mining expedition was the lack of water. In one instance during Ramesses II's reign, the shortage was so severe in the desert regions of Wawat that half the expedition's men and animals died of thirst before they even reached the mines! Well aware that fewer workers meant lower yields, but knowing also that during Sety I's rule, in this same area, miners had dug down 200 feet without finding water, Ramesses II summoned the princes of the court and asked for ideas. His Viceroy of Kush suggested that Ramesses II himself pray to Hapi (god of the Nile flood), "Let water be brought upon the mountain." [19] Hapi would heed Ramesses' plea, the Viceroy assured him, "because all the gods love you more than any king." [20] Recognizing good advice, Ramesses II gave it a try, and behold, a mere 20 feet down, his workers struck water!

After the miners reduced tons of rock to powder from which they retrieved the gold dust, it was smelted into easily transportable units and brought to Egypt in bars, rings or lumps. Scribes carefully weighed and recorded it, and it finally found its way to the treasure houses and workshops of the king and the gods.

Egyptian gold in its natural state ranged between 17 and 22 carats. To produce treasures for the gods or the royal family, or golden gifts for trusted officials who had distinguished themselves in Pharaoh's service, craftsmen melted the gold (at a heat of 1945° Fahrenheit) in a blast furnace fueled by wood and dung and stoked by means of a foot-operated bellows. Goldsmiths then cast the molten metal in molds, hammered it into sheets, drew it out into wire, cut it into strips, formed it into granules (Cat. No. 18) or mixed it with other elements which added color or strength. With solder (made from a copper salt and gum or from a gold alloy) they could produce a joint that was almost invisible (Cat. Nos. 17, 21 and 22). Alternatively, they might use gold rivets (Cat. No. 25). Wielding tiny chisels and mallets, the gold workers engraved, embossed, chased and hammered designs and inscriptions into plain surfaces. They used brightly colored stones or glass set into cloisons (dividing bands) to add interest, to jewelry especially (Cat. No. 18). Beautifully fashioned golden vessels enabled the gods to eat and drink in style (Cat. Nos. 21-25). They fashioned awesome ceremonial weapons, and their sheet gold coverings made temple doors, walls, obelisks and columns glisten.

Delicate and beautiful, masterpieces created by these artisans over 3,000 years ago are as appealing to us today as they must have been to their original owners. The reign of Ramesses the Great, thanks to them, was indeed a golden age.

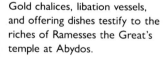

Gold chalices, libation vessels, and offering dishes testify to the riches of Ramesses the Great's temple at Abydos.

Governance of the Kingdom

Ramesses the Great ruled an estimated 3,000,000 people in Egypt proper, and his jurisdiction over Nubia and the Levant added another few million, according to one demographic estimate. The well-being of all his subjects was the king's responsibility, to be fulfilled, in theory, with divine assistance. In practice, he relied on a multi-branched administrative structure established in rudimentary form at the beginning of dynastic Egyptian history (ca. 3200 B.C.).

By Dynasty XIX, the Egyptian administration had evolved into a complex bureaucracy which may be divided into four branches: royal court, temple, military and civil service. Each branch had its own responsibilities and hierarchy, but each reported ultimately to the king. In Ramesses the Great's Egypt, the king always maintained control.

The large palaces Ramesses II built for himself in major cities—Pi-Ramesses, Memphis, Thebes—were far more than just residential quarters. Often they included a complex of government offices, reception areas, archives, storerooms, workrooms, stables, stockyards, breweries, bakeries, kitchens, military marshalling areas, ornamental gardens, pleasure lakes and perhaps a harbor. The king, his wives and children, his trusted officials and their families would have occupied the palace's living areas. Royal lands provided food and income to supplement tribute and taxes. Artisans' studios and cottage industries supplied immediate needs.

Remains of the audience hall and throne room from the palace of Ramesses II at the Ramesseum.

Each palace compound had its own administrative staff. Chief stewards coordinated the efforts of scribes, bakers, brewers, cooks, butlers, gardeners, overseers, farm laborers, herdsmen, stable masters, guards, artisans, nurses, weavers, tutors, messengers and body servants. When the king traveled, his personal entourage included such specialists as cup bearer, sandal bearer, sunshade bearer and fan bearer. (Their duties were probably more ceremonial than physically demanding.)

How splendid these edifices must have been in Ramesses II's day. Since they were intended for use only during the king's life on earth—his eternal dwelling place would be in the Valley of the Kings—they were built mainly of mud brick, an impermanent material. Today little remains, apart from some brightly colored faience tiles, which once adorned the walls and floors of his magnificent palace at Pi-Ramesses (Cat. Nos. 39-43), and stone column bases and mudbrick foundations from a less imposing palace within the sacred precinct of his mortuary temple, the Ramesseum. Ramesses II built certain smaller palaces to serve as short-term resting places so that he could conduct business and receive visitors at select temples such as the Ramesseum (the construction of which had begun almost immediately after his coronation).

Leaning down from the window of appearance, King Sety I presents Hormin with the Gold of Valor necklaces. From Saqqara.

Some clues to the way the royal court functioned are found in the remains of the Ramesseum palace. Though miniscule in comparison to the vast acreage of Ramesses II's major palaces, its layout, displaying a clear division between public and private areas, was probably characteristic of all his residences. Behind a square reception area, filled with 16 columns arranged in rows of four, lay a smaller, square, four-columned room with a dais where the enthroned king might greet high officials. Auxiliary rooms for ritual or storage surrounded the complex. Far to the rear and inaccessible from the public areas lay four small housing units. On ceremonial occasions Ramesses II might ascend a stairway to a balcony overlooking the temple's open court. From this lofty "window of appearance" he could address his subjects or present awards. The Ramesseum palace also played a role in Ramesses II's funeral ceremonies.

Living quarters for great royal wives, lesser wives, children, servants and administrators occupied substantial space within palace districts. The harem was not just a residential area. Here young princes, princesses and children of high officials learned reading, writing, politics and leadership, manners and morals. Foreign princes sent their children here (sometimes unwillingly) to receive training in the Egyptian way of life. Virtually an independent institution, the harem had its own administrative staff and its own cottage industries, including weaving, farming and herding.

While court officials attended to the concerns of the State (i.e., the king), temple personnel similarly cared for the gods and their holdings. Like the State, temples owned fields, gardens, animals, workyards, storehouses, boats, slaves, mineral wealth, even entire market towns, all of which required large administrative and maintenance staffs. Most temple precincts also included wayside chapels, archives, artisans' studios, schools and living quarters.

The high priest of each temple served as its supreme authority in the absence of the king. (The high priest of Amun at Karnak wielded considerable power, since Karnak was one of the main employers in New Kingdom Egypt.) Second, third and fourth priests or prophets aided the high priest in attending to the god's intimate needs. A temple's lesser priests performed other duties, such as reciting liturgy, burning incense, pouring libations, celebrating special festivals, collecting offerings, maintaining records and tracking the passage of time so that each ritual might be performed at its specified day and hour (Cat. No. 15). There were also lay *(wab)* priests

who served for one month at a time, three times a year. During their period of duty, they, like full-time priests, were obliged to shave their entire bodies, refrain from wearing wool clothing and remain sexually abstinent. Women of the New Kingdom aided their gods primarily as singers, dancers and musicians, although occasionally they attained higher priestly office as well. Meryetamun, daughter and later wife of Ramesses II, served as Sistrum Player for Mut, Menat Player for Hathor, Songstress of Atum and Dancer for Horus (Cat. No. 4).

A temple's riches came largely from royal gifts presented by kings to curry divine favor and priestly support. In exchange, kings hoped to obtain what only the gods could give—long life, dominion, health and general prosperity. Over the years a temple might accumulate enormous wealth. By Dynasty XX, for example, fully 10% of Egypt's agricultural land belonged to the sanctuary of Amun at Karnak.

In many respects, houses of gods in Ramesside Egypt resembled semi-autonomous corporations. One temple might lease land to another or open it to sharecroppers. Temple-owned ships transported goods from its market towns. Surpluses might be traded, but despite their vast power, temple priests remained subordinate to the king. Before any income in the form of produce, grain, wines, oil, precious stones and metals, cloth and handiwork went into temple storerooms, a share went to the king as tax. Not even the gods were exempt!

To ensure that the king's voice would remain supreme was the task of the military. A standing army had existed in Egypt only since the beginning of the New Kingdom (ca. 1550 B.C.), when it was established to protect newly conquered territories. By Dynasty XIX, it had grown considerably.

The king was indisputable commander-in-chief of the army, and we know Ramesses II took his role seriously. Generals, usually princes, commanded each division of about 5000 men and reported to the king. Each division, consisting of infantry and chariotry regiments of about 200 to 250 men under the leadership of a commander or standard bearer, was further subdivided into platoons of 50. The smallest units of his army were squads of ten men each.

To recruit troops for the army's mainstay, the infantry, army scribes traveled from village to village promising young farm boys adventure, foreign plunder and a chance to better their lot if they became soldiers. Teachers, meanwhile, fearful that children of noble families might also be seduced into joining the army, instructed their pupils about the reality of a military life. According to a New Kingdom papyrus: "The soldier, that much tormented one...is taken when yet a child to be imprisoned in a barrack."[21] In training, "he is beaten like papyrus and battered with castigation."[22] On the march, "his bread and water are upon his shoulder like the load of an ass...he drinks of smelly water and halts (only) to keep watch."[23] In battle, "he is like a plucked bird...Turn back," the teachers warned, "from the soldier's calling."[24] When army recruiters failed to produce sufficient inductees for Pharaoh's army, they resorted to conscription. Foreign mercenaries and prisoners of war also joined the ranks of the military.

Ramesses II's troops fought valiantly for him (most of the time). Archers led the way into battle, followed by soldiers armed with axes, swords, daggers and spears and protected by shields, helmets and sometimes coats of mail. Chariots, made of wood with bronze and leather trappings, protected each flank and the rear. Charioteers

Ramesses II's High Priest of Amun Bakenkhonsu. He probably usurped this statue from an official of Dynasty XVIII. From Karnak.

were the army's elite. Each two-wheeled chariot was pulled by two horses and carried two men. Generally, one man drove as the other fought with bow and arrow or spear, but an especially valiant driver might tie the reins around his body and battle beside his companion.

When Egypt was at peace, Ramesses the Great's soldiers lived well, served as an internal police force, patroled the borders, manned foreign garrisons and labored on public works. Whether stationed at home or abroad, they enjoyed a varied diet of meat, fowl, vegetables, bread, oil and, of course, beer and wine. Those who had served bravely received further rewards—enemy plunder, grants of land, office and, if they had truly distinguished themselves, possibly even the Gold of Valor (Cat. No. 26).

Court officials, priests, and regiment commanders played their roles, but it was Ramesses II's civil service bureaucrats who kept Egypt and her conquered territories functioning. Egypt's two viziers, presiding from Memphis for Lower Egypt and from Thebes for Upper Egypt (Cat. No. 33), were the most powerful officials in the land. They directed all public services and public works, ensured that all civil government branches worked together efficiently and maintained open communication with the royal court, the priesthood and the military, no small task in Ramesses II's day. Appointment to this high office theoretically was made solely on the basis of ability, but family connections probably played a greater role. The Southern Vizier, Paser, for instance, who was appointed by Sety I and went on to serve some 25 years into Ramesses II's reign, was the son of a high priest of Amun.

Paser, in an inscription on the wall of his tomb—he copied it from the tomb of a Dynasty XVIII vizier who, in turn, had usurped a Middle Kingdom text—left us an account of his job. It sounds very much like that of any modern day chief executive officer. Each day, ideally, began with a policy meeting with Ramesses II and a conference with the royal steward. Then Paser met with his own staff of deputies, overseers, mayors, heralds, scribes and treasurers, listened to their accounts and issued orders. He signed legal contracts, maintained archives, inspected construction projects, established property boundaries, organized labor on canals, fields and tombs, received official delegations, provided police protection, oversaw workshops, supervised commerce and communication and officiated at festivals.

The vizier, in the name of the king and in his role as judge, presided over the high courts or *kenbets*, which convened at Memphis and Thebes. These councils, using plaintiff-defendant procedures remarkably similar to ours, decided grave criminal cases and major civil disputes. Local *kenbets* dealt with lesser problems—property disputes, payments, inheritances, charges of adultery and minor criminal offenses. Meticulous accounts on these trials suggest that they were lively village events enjoyed by all.

Ramesses II's administration, like that of any modern day government, relied on taxes to fund State institutions, and it was the vizier's responsibility to oversee tax

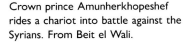

Crown prince Amunherkhopeshef rides a chariot into battle against the Syrians. From Beit el Wali.

Workers measure grain for taxes. From the tomb of Ipy at Deir el Medina.

collection. Fishermen, farmers and herdsmen delivered their shares to city mayors, as scribes kept careful account for the vizier. The vizier's treasury officials collected levies from craftsmen and even priests. Farm produce and manufactured goods were surveyed yearly, and a percentage of all crops and products went to Pharaoh's stores. Large landowners were assessed, percentage-wise, a larger "harvest tax" than small farmers. The system appears fair, but ancient records show that disgruntled citizens lodged occasional complaints, such as this one: "What is this wrong you are doing to me? It is I (alone) whom you have found to penalize amongst the entire body of tax-payers." [25] The result of his plea remains unknown.

In the end, much of Egypt's wealth returned to her citizens directly and indirectly, because the economy was based on a redistribution system. All those who worked for Ramesses II—soldiers, quarrymen, builders, craftsmen, government officials—received their wages in the form of food and drink, clothing and household effects. The abundant food and free-flowing beverages the public enjoyed at many temple festivals also came from Pharaoh's stores. Thanks to the bounty of the land, hunger was rare in the Egypt of Ramesses the Great.

The Life of the People

In comparison with many other ancient civilizations, we know a great deal about Egypt. This is due, in part, to the Egyptians' delight in life and their desire to continue enjoying life's earthly pleasures in the netherworld. They equipped their tombs with all the material requirements for a blissful existence. Their tomb wall paintings depict them engaged in activities chosen to guarantee them pleasure, nourishment and divine favor in the afterlife. They often recorded the events of their lives in tomb inscriptions which can now be read, thanks to the work of Jean François Champollion, the early nineteenth century French linguist. He, with others, established the principles for deciphering Egyptian hieroglyphics.

Other sources of information about how and where the ancient Egyptians lived are diverse—sociologists, anthropologists, palaeobotanists, scholars of military and religious history, even geographers and climatologists. Geography and climate, no less than commercial needs, political requirements and divine dictates, influenced the location and development of farms, villages, cities, trade routes, industrial centers, strategic defense areas and sacred ground.

The amount of Egypt's land devoted to agriculture in Dynasty XIX has been estimated to be as high as 5,500,000 acres. The size of a New Kingdom family farm was about three and one third acres. Some farmers worked fields in return for a share of their yield. Soldiers, who served their king valiantly, received gifts of land from state or temple holdings, the standard being approximately two acres.

As soon as flood waters subsided (August at Aswan, as late as October elsewhere), farmers hitched cows and oxen to heavy wooden plows and broke up the fertile earth. Most sowed seeds of barley, emmer and flax, New Kingdom Egypt's main crops, and carefully tended them over the next four months or so. At harvest time, they lopped off the heads of grain with sickles and brought them to the threshing floor where cattle trampled them to break open the husks. Workers then tossed them in the air with winnowing spoons. The wind took the chaff. What was left was gathered into

Sennedjem plows and his wife
scatters seed in a painting from their
tomb at Deir el Medina.

Sennedjem cuts grain with a sickle,
and his wife collects the ears in her
basket. From Deir el Medina.

heaps, measured, recorded and returned to farmers, less the amount due tax assessors. Flax plants had to be harvested near the root so the precious fibers would not suffer damage. After seeds were detached for next years' planting, the stalks were transformed into linen thread from which was woven the cloth most commonly worn by Egyptians, rich and poor. (In the hot Egyptian climate, wool was too warm, and silk and cotton came to Egypt only in Ptolemaic and Roman times respectively.)

Even with the land's fertility guaranteed yearly by the silt-bearing flood waters, the lot of the farmer was difficult. One late New Kingdom school text asked young readers to consider the plight of the "cultivator" in whose fields "mice abound, the locust descends, the cattle devour (and) sparrows bring want" and who still had to pay his harvest-tax "after the snake has carried off one-half and the hippopotamus has eaten up the rest." [26]

On desert fringes beyond the agricultural lands, lay animal grazing land. Oxen and cattle, bulls, pigs, sheep, goats and donkeys were raised for work and for food. Animals less domestic, including ibex, oryx, gazelle and antelope might also be trapped for game parks and the gods' offering tables. Wild fowl—at least 14 species have been identified—were captured and raised for food and for aviaries of wealthy estate owners. In addition, New Kingdom Egypt witnessed the arrival of the domestic chicken. Imagine an owner's delight, watching these wonderful birds lay an egg every day!

Farms and herds fed and clothed Egypt's people, but towns and cities, located usually on the floodplain but high enough to escape flood waters, formed her cultural hubs. A few cities were planned, among them Tell el Amarna, Pi-Ramesses, Nubian garrison areas and Deir el Medina, a village near the Valley of the Kings built to provide homes for workmen constructing the royal tombs. These planned cities often display an axial layout of streets and houses, with various sectors devoted to separate concentrations of administrative buildings, temples, crafts and industries, markets or living quarters. Most towns, however, spread irregularly on the basis of need and availability of land. In many instances, they grew up around the estates their inhabitants served.

In residential areas, larger houses were grouped together in affluent "suburbs," while smaller domiciles in poorer sections shared contiguous walls. Most families had to make do with modest mudbrick dwellings of three or four rooms laid out one behind the other, like the typical Deir el Medina home. A foyer, entered from the street, led to a larger room with a low platform to one side for eating or sleeping and a false door stela for worship set into the wall. One or two plastered wood columns supported a flat wooden roof, and light was admitted through tiny windows just below the ceiling. A short flight of steps led down to a household storage area. Behind the "living room" lay a sleeping area containing a bed niche. Food was prepared on the roof or at the rear of the house in an open air "kitchen" which generally contained a clay oven and a recessed mortar for grinding grain. Throughout the house, plastered mudbrick floors and walls might be painted with images of favorite deities, floral friezes or simple bands of color.

On the whole, furniture was sparse and utilitarian. People sat on high- or low-back chairs and stools and ate at low tables from a variety of plates, bowls, saucers, pitchers and cups made primarily of undecorated, wheel-thrown pottery. At night, reed mats or beds with woven cord "springs" provided comfort. Padded headrests

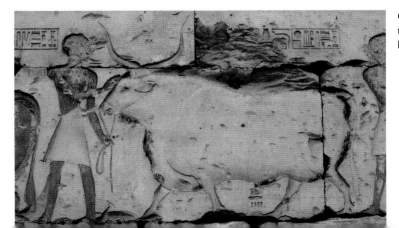

Cattle grew fat from the bounty of the land. From the temple of Ramesses II at Abydos.

Padded reed mats placed in niches often served as beds for Deir el Medina villagers.

Deir el Medina kitchens included sunken hearths for cooking. Walls throughout the houses were often plastered and white-washed.

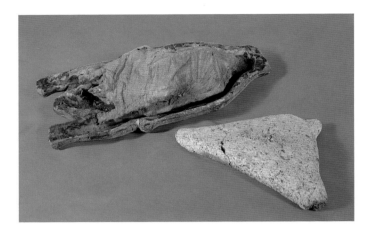

Triangular bread loaf and trussed duck in a case.

Villagers trap a rich variety of fish in Nile waters. From the tomb of Ipy at Deir el Medina.

served as pillows (Cat. No. 38). Baskets and wooden chests (Cat. No. 36) stored linen and personal articles. Often, clever methods of construction, veneering, inlay and painting made inexpensive woods more attractive. Acacia and sycamore, commonly used in furniture, were available locally, but the more highly prized cedar and ebony had to be imported from Lebanon and Nubia respectively. Most families made their own simple furniture, but they might commission more ornate or elaborate pieces from local carpenters in exchange for other goods or services.

To ancient Egyptians, corpulence was synonymous with prosperity. Because workmen were paid largely in food, wage records, together with actual food remains and paintings of food on tomb walls, provide us with information about their diet. Bread and beer were its primary components. Loaves of bread, formed in many different shapes and using a variety of ingredients such as honey, milk, fruit, eggs and fats, were baked in cylindrical ovens, on low braziers or over open fires. In Ramesses the Great's Egypt, over 40 words existed for breads and cakes! Villagers made their own beer by mixing, baking and fermenting the basic ingredients—barley, yeast and malt—in several stages of preparation. The alcoholic content of the resulting beverage, up to 8.1%, was greater than today's brews (6%). Regular beer was enjoyed daily, but for festivals its flavor might be enhanced with honey, mint, pomegranate, figs or grapes.

Among the vegetables Egyptians ate were lettuce, cucumbers, celery, melons, onions, leeks, garlic and beans. Fish appears to have been their main protein source.

Such varieties as bolti fish (Cat. Nos. 41, 53 and 67), mullet (Cat. No. 42), catfish, mormyr and perch (sometimes so large it took two men to carry them) were caught in traps, nets and on hooks. Scaled and cleaned, they might be sun-dried, broiled, baked or boiled with vegetables in savory stews. Also important to the diet were oils and fats. Oil from the castor bean was the cheapest and most prevalent; sesame and moringa oils and animal fats were also used. For festivals or as bonuses, workmen sometimes received gourmet fare—wine, milk, meat, fowl, fruit or condiments awarded from royal stores or temple treasuries.

For some in Ramesses the Great's Egypt—the palace official, the priest, the scribe—life could be most pleasant. They lived in style, educated their children well, dressed fashionably and generally enjoyed the amenities of a prosperous cosmopolitan society.

In crowded cities houses for the wealthy might be multi-storied structures with each level devoted to a separate function. Work areas, storage and servants' quarters occupied the ground floor; the first floor consisted of large public reception areas; above were bedrooms and a roof terrace where food was prepared. In the "suburbs" the elite lived in luxurious, sprawling estates that testified to the prosperity of their owners. One such home was described by its owner as "a goodly villa...on the verge (of the river)...planted with trees on every side," and boasting "fine door-posts of limestone inscribed and carved...and walls inlaid with lapis lazuli." [27] Its splendors did not stop at the house doors, for it had granaries "packed with abundance, a fowl-yard and an aviary...a breeding bird-pool; horses (are) in the stable...ferry boats and new cattle boats are moored at its quay...fishes are more plentiful than the sand of the riverbanks." [28]

A special benefit enjoyed by heirs of the elite was education. At the age of five, young boys from noble families began studies at "schools" connected with the royal court, temples and government institutions. Under a teacher's watchful eye, they mastered both cursive hieratic, the script of routine correspondence, and the more formal and artistic hieroglyphic writing.

The classics of Egyptian literature served as models not only for grammar and spelling but also for virtue and moral principles: "Do not give your heart to pleasures," young students were warned, "or you shall be a failure. Write with your hand, read with your mouth, and take advice of those who know more than you." [29] Teachers also offered their pupils career counseling—in this example, based on experience: "Be a scribe. It saves you from toil...and spares you torment, as you are not under many lords and numerous masters." [30] Additionally, they pointed out: "He who works in writing is not taxed. Take note of this." [31] Clearly, the scribal profession was the key to success in Ramesses the Great's Egypt.

The Egyptians took pleasure in attractive attire and personal adornment. The undyed linen that villagers used to make clothing was generally woven by women on two-beamed horizontal ground looms and graded into categories on the basis of the number of threads per unit. Royal linen, the best they produced, was even finer than today's delicate handkerchiefs.

For work, men wore simple, wrapped kilts, but on more festive occasions they donned bag tunics made by folding a large rectangle of linen in half, hemming it up the sides to the armhole and cutting a circle in the center for the head. A second

Servant women wash clothing at Deir el Medina. From the tomb of Ipy.

piece of linen wrapped around the torso and knotted in front created an apron-like effect (Cat. No. 62). For added warmth, sleeves might be sewn in, and on the coldest nights, a shawl provided further protection. Sandals of leather or woven papyrus and, perhaps, a walking stick completed the costume.

Stylish women of Dynasty XIX wore floor-length dresses made of linen rectangles draped around their torsos and over their shoulders, knotted beneath their breasts and trimmed with fringed borders and pleats secured with sizing (Cat. No. 63). Tomb paintings suggest that these garments were often transparent, billowy and as elegant as the occasions for which they were designed.

Wealthy Egyptians feasted at sumptuous multi-course banquets, became intoxicated on fine wines and enjoyed lithe dancers performing to the accompaniment of orchestras (Cat. Nos. 55 and 56). They strolled in verdant pleasure gardens filled with exotic trees and shrubs. Colorful flowers surrounded artificial ponds suitable for boating or bathing. Board games provided further entertainment (Cat. Nos. 58, 59 and 72), and, as in life itself, the stakes were high. Fate, in theory, was the opponent; eternal life was the winner's prize.

Most Egyptians cut their hair short with bronze razors (Cat. No. 50) or flint knives. Outside the house men and women of high station wore wigs woven from strands of natural human hair, each secured individually to a matrix by means of resin and beeswax and kept neat by combs (Cat. No. 51). A lump of scented fat placed atop a wig would melt under the heat of the sun and prevent the hair from becoming brittle. (It must have also contributed a pungent aroma as it aged.) For wrinkles, for dandruff and for all manner of ills and injuries, Egyptian medical papyri prescribed cures, and skilled doctors were available for hire. Jewels of gold, silver and precious stones added allure to the appearance of those who could afford them (Cat. Nos. 18-20). Others less fortunate made do with ancient Egypt's equivalent of costume jewelry fashioned from brightly glazed faience. Colorful multi-rowed floral collars, delicate single-strand necklaces, beaded bracelets and armbands and gaudy rings in multiples stood out against the white of the Egyptians' linen garments.

No respectable man or woman of Ramesses the Great's day would have appeared in public without proper make-up. Kohl made from galena to outline the eyes and shield them from the sun's glare (Cat. Nos. 46-48), red ochre mixed with fat to redden the cheeks and perhaps the lips, and creams to keep skin soft and supple transformed an ordinary countenance into one of great beauty. Mirrors were available to inspect the results (Cat. No. 49).

Dressed in their finest linen garments, wearing their long elegant wigs, adorned with jewels, painted with cosmetics and scented with floral perfumes, Ramesside high society's beauties must have rivaled those of any culture in any age.

Ipy and his wife, elegantly dressed in Ramesside high fashion, receive offerings from their children. Copy of a painting from their tomb at Deir el Medina (substantially restored).

Desolate cliffs in the Valley of the Kings hid the tombs of New Kingdom royalty.

III
Quest for Immortality

To ancient Egyptians, an ideal life on earth lasted 110 years. If proper conditions were met, death was not an end but a beginning—the start of a journey into an other-worldly realm of everlasting bliss. Ramesses the Great, living well into his ninth decade, was on his way to achieving the ideal, for he had expended considerable resources and manpower to guarantee his immortality.

Early in his reign, he had begun to make careful preparations for his death, burial and entry into eternity to join his fellow gods. Like his New Kingdom predecessors, Ramesses chose sites in Western Thebes for the majestic mortuary temple where his funeral ceremonies were to be held and for the royal tomb where he would be buried. Heeding lessons learned millennia earlier, he located his temple, the Ramesseum, at the desert's edge, on the opposite side of the limestone cliffs from the *wadi*, known as the Valley of the Kings, where his tomb would be hidden. This was to draw attention away from his burial place and ensure its security against violation and plunder. Or so he thought. Work on both temple and tomb began almost immediately after Ramesses II assumed the throne.

Looking down the papyrus columns of the hypostyle hall at the Ramesseum.

The king's cult lived on in his funerary temple, the Ramesseum.

An Eternal Dwelling Place

The Ramesseum was designed to be a splendid eternal dwelling place where the cult of the king would be honored in perpetuity. The spot Ramesses chose to build this "House of Millions of Years United with Thebes," as the Ramesseum was called in his day, lay on the edge of the desert between the temples of Kings Amunhotep II and Tuthmosis IV of Dynasty XVIII. Here he erected not only a temple, which reproduced elements of Karnak on a smaller scale, but also a palace, storerooms and housing for his funerary priests. The magazines or warehouses of the Ramesseum provide some idea of the size and complexity of this enterprise. The area of the enclosed temple precinct devoted to storage of commodities was three times that allotted to the temple itself. There were 20 large, vaulted, mudbrick granaries, each of which held sufficient barley and emmer wheat to feed 60 families for more than two years. Similarly, great amounts of other goods, like wine, honey and oil, filled smaller storerooms.

In the Ramesseum temple area proper, a massive stone pylon opened onto an open-air court flanked on the north and south by pillars and columns. Dominating this court and, indeed, the entire temple was a 66-foot-high, 1000-ton seated statue of Ramesses, with an inscription which, according to ancient Greek translators, proclaimed him the King of Kings. A stairway led to a second open-air colonnaded court where additional towering statues of the king, this time represented as Osiris, god of resurrection, flanked pillars on the east and west sides. From the second court, a 48-columned hypostyle hall, second in size only to Karnak's, led to three smaller columned halls and finally to a sanctuary in the rear.

Nowhere in Egypt are ancient storerooms better preserved than at the Ramesseum. The largest, which were granaries, were filled through holes in the roof and emptied through side doors.

The Ramesseum was oriented to the Luxor temple on the east bank of the Nile so that during the annual "Beautiful Feast of the Valley" celebrations (Cat. No. 11), the god Amun might travel in his royal barque across the river and visit Ramesses the Great's funerary temple. Here in the "House of Millions of Years," the dead king and the god would become one.

As one group of builders and artisans was constructing the Ramesseum, a second group worked on Ramesses the Great's tomb. Their task involved carving and decorating the tomb according to precise specifications so that the king's resurrection and rebirth would be assured. The Ramesseum was essentially completed by Year 20 based on the early spelling of the king's name which changed slightly from Thebes to Nubia after Year 20.

This select group of approximately 50 artisans and supervisors reported directly to the vizier. They lived in Deir el Medina, a village in Western Thebes founded in early Dynasty XVIII to provide convenient living quarters for royal tomb builders and their families. By the time of Ramesses II's rule, the village had grown considerably in size and prosperity. Inside a protective wall, about 70 houses were grouped in contiguous units along two main avenues. Gates at the north and south ends excluded those who did not belong. Around the village lay its temples, tombs and tomb chapels. Total population is estimated to have been around 300.

Excavators at Deir el Medina have uncovered a wealth of domestic and archival material as yet unsurpassed in amount and state of preservation. Remains from the village, including the "Journal of the Necropolis," a day-to-day account written on ostraca about the mundane trivialities of work at the tomb, provide a window to the inner workings of an ancient enterprise. Work schedules, equipment, delivery of sup-

Pillagers and an earthquake reduced the Ramesseum to a ruin. Although now only a shadow of its former magnificence, the statue to the right is one of the largest ever carved from a single block of stone.

Following page. The second court of the Ramesseum with statues of the King. His crossed arms holding crook and flail and mummiform body identify him as Osiris, god of resurrection.

One of the main streets at Deir el Medina. Houses shared side walls.

Debris from repeated floods now fills the burial chamber in the tomb of Ramesses the Great.

plies, excuses for skipping work, rewards and punishments, promotions and interactions between management and staff, all dating back more than 3,000 years, may be viewed as if they took place today. For example, Deir el Medina records show that a workman's basic monthly wage (received ideally on the twenty-eighth day) was four 76 liter sacks of emmer for bread and one and one-half sacks of barley to make beer. This amount would have comfortably nourished a family of ten.

The artisans who worked on Ramesses the Great's tomb were divided into two groups or gangs. Because of attractive work schedules and generous compensation, places on the gangs were in great demand. Generally son succeeded father, often generation after generation, and bribery of officials to assure an appointment was not unknown. A foreman, assisted by a deputy, headed each gang, supervising their performance, monitoring progress, supplying equipment, resolving disputes and representing their interests to the vizier. A scribe, who also reported to the vizier, maintained the daily log, registered supplies, wrote letters and compiled reports. Although, strictly speaking, they were not members of the ''gang,'' Doorkeepers of the Tomb maintained round-the-clock security.

Probably it was the vizier, accompanied by stone masons and architects, who selected an appropriate spot in the Valley for the king's tomb—subject to royal approval, of course. The tomb which housed the mortal remains of Ramesses the Great is located near the entrance to the Valley of the Kings (Royal Tomb #7). In layout and decoration, it largely reproduced earlier royal sepulchers of Dynasty XIX. It deviated from them only in incorporating one right-angle turn, rather than a straight axis, in the passageway leading to the vaulted burial chamber. This design may have been prompted by an intrusive bed of shale that experienced stone carvers thought safest to avoid.

Construction was carefully planned. First, quarrymen cut diagonally down into the soft limestone with heavy copper or bronze chisels. Others followed with plumb bobs and right angle levels (Cat. Nos. 31 and 32), smoothing any unevenness with precision tools. Plasterers patched flaws and covered the naked rock with a layer of gypsum. Next, draughtsmen laid out registers with the aid of a cubit rod (Cat. No. 30) and filled them with inscriptions and decorations painted in red ink. Then, carvers slowly and carefully cut down the background area, making figures and text stand out in raised relief. Finally, painters covered the reliefs using a rich palette of natural earth tones. Presumably, the stone cutters and painters took turns working, since the fine dust raised by the chisels would have rendered the pigments unusable.

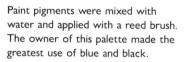

Paint pigments were mixed with water and applied with a reed brush. The owner of this palette made the greatest use of blue and black.

Ramesses II makes an offering to a goddess in a representation from his tomb.

The artisans probably worked a four-hour shift in the morning and a similar stint in the afternoon. One gang may have been responsible for the right side of the tomb and the other for the left. We know the tomb was cut and decorated one room at a time so that in the event of an unexpected royal death, it would be usable with some hasty finishing touches. When the gangs ceased work each day, their valuable copper and bronze tools were collected for sharpening and safekeeping. (One copper chisel cost more than a family's grain supply for a month.) The State also kept a record of the linen wicks and lamp oil it issued.

In theory, for eight days out of ten, the artisans cut and painted Ramesses II's tomb, spending nights in temporary huts overlooking the Valley and going home to Deir el Medina only on their days off. In practice, they took far more time off for such "legitimate" reasons as beer brewing, drinking sessions, house building and repair, moonlighting for their superiors, work on their own tombs, family quarrels, festivals, personal or family illness, parental visits and family rites of passage including births and deaths. By Year 40 of Ramesses II's reign, some men were working an average of only one day out of four! (Only two men that year maintained a perfect attendance record.) Presumably the vizier permitted such laxity because work on the king's tomb was largely finished by that time.

Excluding its end halls, Ramesses II's tomb measures 324 feet in length, a large tomb by New Kingdom standards, although not the largest. In quality, the tomb of Ramesses the Great, with its delicately modeled, low relief representations and its finely carved hieroglyphs, is unsurpassed. Proficient as they were, however, the Deir el Medina artisans still made mistakes, in one instance even spelling the king's name incorrectly. A layer of plaster was applied to cover the blunder, but it has since fallen off.

Head of Osiris, god of resurrection, from the tomb of Ramesses the Great.

Death of a King

After some 66 years and two months of sole rule over the world's most powerful country, Ramesses the Great departed this earth. His death came sometime during the Second month of the season of *Akhet* (August), 1213 B.C. Most likely in his eighties at the time, he suffered from arthritis severe enough to cause him to stoop and from dental abscesses which undoubtedly generated constant pain. Old age was the probable cause of his death, which seems to have occurred while he was in residence at his Delta capital, Pi-Ramesses. (We know the preparation of his body took place in the Delta, and logically in or near Pi-Ramesses, since some of the sand found in the mummy came from a marine rather than a riverine environment.) Immediate steps were taken to preserve Ramesses II's body through mummification so that his soul would be housed eternally. Essentially, mummification is a process of desiccation, or drying out. (The word "mummy" comes from the Arabic "mummiya," meaning bitumen, a gummy black material which resembles embalming resins.) The process took 70 days, the same length of time that the bright star Sirius remained beneath the horizon before it reappeared again, rising just before dawn.

We may conjecture that Ramesses II's body was carried to the House of Embalming, placed on a long wooden table and cleansed with the Nile's life-giving water. Mortuary priests, chanting ancient prayers, then made a cut in his left side and removed from both abdominal and thoracic cavities the internal organs which might cause his body to decompose. His liver, lungs, stomach and intestines were retained and treated separately. Generally, the heart was left in place, but Ramesses II's heart was removed and sewn back in later with golden thread. (We know this from the recent examination of Ramesses II's mummy performed at the Louis Pasteur Institute in Paris.) Chanted spells helped ensure the heart's safety. As the source of intellect and feeling, according to ancient Egyptian thought, its preservation was critical since it contained a record of all Ramesses II's actions and was required in his final judgment. Only if his heart were no heavier than the feather of truth *(Ma'at)*, would he be granted eternal life. In contrast, little significance was attached to Ramesses II's brain, so, in keeping with New Kingdom tradition, it was cut up and drawn out in pieces through his nose. Funerary priests then poured wine, scented with aromatic spices, inside his empty body cavity to cleanse it. Embalmers temporarily packed the body with bulky absorbent materials—wads of linen containing bits of straw, sand, natron and resins—to preserve its shape and hasten the drying process.

About 16 days later, mortuary priests laid the king's body out on a slanted bed and covered it with the principal drying agent in mummification, powdered natron, a naturally occurring salt found in Wadi Natrun near the Western Delta. There the body remained for the next 40 days, after which time its weight would have decreased approximately 75% through loss of water.

Following its natron bath, embalmers emptied the king's body of its temporary stuffing, washed it and dried it. Then, as lector priests recited the appropriate texts, bandagers began the critical task of permanently packing and wrapping Ramesses II's body. Embalmers lined the inside of the body cavity with cloth of yellow and blue, the colors of gold and lapis lazuli. (Traces were found adhering to the ribs.) They inserted peppercorns in the king's nostrils—probably to help them keep their shape and also to reawaken his sense of smell—and stuffed his body cavity with undyed linen soaked in resin. Other important ingredients of the packing materials included bits of wood (cypress mainly, but also fir and oak), pollen from a variety of flowers (including sage, linden and camomile), wild tobacco, fragments of the bulb of the narcissus flower and undoubtedly myriad other special substances now gone. All of these were intended to preserve and revitalize the body.

Packing complete, the incision on Ramesses II's left side was closed, and priests turned their attention to treating the exterior. To keep his skin supple, they massaged it with unguents and oils. At some point henna, thought to have rejuvenative qualities because of its blood-like color, was applied to the king's hair (coincidentally approximating the natural auburn color of his youth). Priests crossed his hands over his chest, placing left over right (a reversal of the standard royal position), and the bandagers, with sheets, strips and wads of linen in readiness, began wrapping Ramesses the Great's body.

Although none of the original wrappings remain, it is likely the bandagers began by dressing the king in a golden-colored linen shroud. After carefully wrapping each finger and toe separately (and then perhaps covering them with individual guards of gold), they next would have bandaged each arm and leg. While lector priests chanted prayers and uttered spells, bandagers continued to wind layer after layer of linen around Ramesses the Great's mortal remains, coating each layer with resins to help stiffen the body. Altogether, several hundred yards of linen must have gone into wrapping Ramesses II's body. Magical amulets were undoubtedly included among the wrappings. Some, imitating body parts, were to ensure that the mummy's corresponding element functioned properly. Others were shaped like animals, reptiles or insects whose salient characteristics, such as strength, tenacity or fertility, might thus be transferred to the body. A large scarab (valued for its seemingly self-regenerative abilities) was presumably laid atop Ramesses II's heart to guarantee him a favorable final judgment. Jewels, some with amuletic significance and others purely decorative, adorned his neck, wrists and fingers.

As the final step in the wrapping process, a shroud about 15 feet long and 4 feet wide and painted with an image of Osiris, god of resurrection, was probably placed over Ramesses II's body, knotted at the ends and secured with linen strips. All the embalmers' refuse—scraps of linen, bits and pieces of entrails, left-over embalming unguents and anything which might have touched the royal remains—was carefully swept up and sealed in jars to be buried near the king's tomb. This, too, was sacred and contained life-giving powers.

At this point, priests undoubtedly covered Ramesses the Great's head and shoulders with a golden mask. Then, they might have carefully lowered his body into a solid gold coffin of anthropoid shape, which was then probably nested inside one or two other coffins also made of gold or gilded wood and possibly inlaid with precious stones. Depictions of the king on the coffin lids probably featured him in different stages of rebirth. Finally, a large granite sarcophagus, carved in an oval shape so that it resembled a cartouche, would have housed the nested coffins.

The king's liver, lungs, stomach and intestines, removed at the start of the mummification process, were cleansed, anointed and wrapped like the rest of the body. Each of the organs fell under the guardianship of one of the four sons of the god Horus, and their images formed the lids of the four canopic jars in which the organs were stored. Alternatively, the lids may have depicted images of their owners (Cat. No. 3).

The internal organs of Ramesses II's royal scribe and chief lector priest, Thenry, were stored inside this set of canopic jars.

Head of the mummy of Ramesses II.

Priests wrapped Ramesses II's toes individually as one of the first steps of the bandaging process.

The god Osiris holds the crook and flail of rulership. His mummiform body reflects his role as master of the netherworld. From the tomb of Sennedjem at Deir el Medina.

Journey to the Netherworld

Seventy days following Ramesses II's arrival at the House of Embalming, mortuary personnel placed his mummified body on a royal barque for its slow journey upriver to Western Thebes. There a bevy of officials, headed by the Southern vizier, had been making preparations for the royal burial. All that the king would need in his afterlife—food and drink, furniture, personal items, ritual objects—had to be ready for the funeral ceremonies since all of it would accompany the king to the tomb.

Some two to three weeks after departing Pi-Ramesses, the barque bearing the royal remains pulled up along the East Bank of the Nile at Thebes. We can imagine how, as evening approached, the royal barque, accompanied by barques of the official burial party, slowly crossed the river following the westward course of the setting sun. Leading the procession that formed when they reached the West Bank was Merneptah, son and successor of Ramesses II. It was his responsibility to bury his father, just as the god Horus had first performed this rite for his father, Osiris. Osiris, rejuvenated, then ruled the netherworld, and Horus inherited his kingdom on earth. Similarly, if correct rituals were observed, Ramesses the Great would become Osiris and rule a netherworld kingdom, and only then could Merneptah become Horus, Egypt's earthly ruler.

En route to the mortuary temple and royal tomb, the king's body in its coffins traveled on a sledge pulled by oxen across the cultivated area that lay between the river and the desert necropolis. A second sledge carried Ramesses II's canopic chest. Merneptah, the Southern vizier, other high dignitaries, along with various priests, offering bearers and professional mourners, wailing and tearing their hair, accompanied the coffins. Priests, preceding them, sprinkled milk along the route as a libation to the gods and sweetened the air with incense. Actresses impersonating the goddesses Nephthys and Isis, Osiris' sisters and wife, walked with the corpse as mourners and guardians at this critical moment prior to burial.

When the procession drew near the tomb, ritual dancers, whirling and snapping their fingers, came to meet them. Then, with participants gathered, a priest wearing

A priest wearing the jackal mask of Anubis, guardian of the necropolis, attends the mummy of Sennedjem in a painting from his tomb at Deir el Medina.

A set of ritual implements used in the Opening of the Mouth ceremony. From the tomb of Ipy at Deir el Medina.

The mummy of Ramesses the Great now at rest in the Cairo Museum.

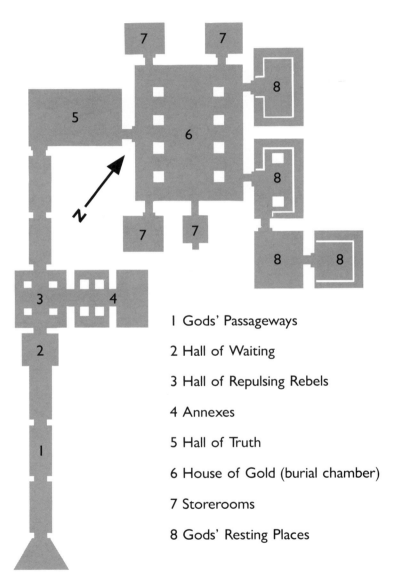

1 Gods' Passageways

2 Hall of Waiting

3 Hall of Repulsing Rebels

4 Annexes

5 Hall of Truth

6 House of Gold (burial chamber)

7 Storerooms

8 Gods' Resting Places

**Tomb of Ramesses the Great
No. 7 in the Valley of the Kings**

the jackal mask of the god Anubis, guardian of the necropolis, embraced the mummy. As a lector priest recited verses and other priests poured libations and burned incense, Merneptah, dressed in a leopard skin in his role as *sem* priest, performed the important rituals of the "Opening of the Mouth" ceremony. He touched his dead father's eyes, nose, mouth and ears with ritual implements, including an adze, a chisel, a snake staff and a bull's right foreleg, so that his senses would be restored to him. This act would enable Ramesses to partake of life's earthly pleasures eternally and also make it possible for his soul to come and go freely.

Traditionally, the final event before the dead king was placed in his house of eternity was a grand funerary banquet held outside the tomb. Dressed in fine floral garlands, the funeral's chief participants enjoyed such delicacies as meat, fowl, cakes, breads and fruits, washed down with beer and fine wines, as priests read prayers to enable the king to feast similarly at every future meal. Then, priests eased Ramesses II's body, in its coffins, down into the burial chamber and put it in the heavy stone sarcophagus which had been placed there earlier.

Since the tomb's passageways and chambers reproduced the nightly path of the sun as it traveled underground to the eastern horizon each morning, the tomb itself held the potential for life. As the sun was reborn daily, so too would the king, identified with the sun, achieve rebirth and rejuvenation.

The text of the funerary ceremonies which took place outside were inscribed on the walls of the tomb in the order they would be needed by the king for his resurrection. Four corridors cut at an incline, the "God's Passageways," led down to a roughly square room which was really a well to foil intruders. The corridor walls contained, first, a text known as the "Litany of Ra," a series of 74 names and praises of the sun god that served as a welcoming greeting to the king and the sun god as they began their trip in their heavenly barque. This text was followed by the start of the *Amduat,* or "Book of What is in the Netherworld," which represented the journey itself, divided into 12 night hours. Each hour corresponded to a challenge the king had to overcome in his quest for immortality, and the text included specific instructions on how to do so. Stars appropriately decorated the ceilings of the passageways. The floor was largely a stairway with a central ramp for sliding the massive stone sarcophagus.

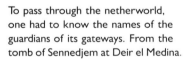

To pass through the netherworld, one had to know the names of the guardians of its gateways. From the tomb of Sennedjem at Deir el Medina.

Upon reaching the square chamber or well, known as the "Hall of Waiting," the royal mummy halted briefly, perhaps for ritual purposes, before proceeding to the four-pillared "Chariot Hall," also called the "Hall of Repulsing Rebels." Here, the demons of the netherworld met their demise. The walls of the next two passages were inscribed with the familiar texts and rites used in the "Opening of the Mouth" ceremony which had to be accomplished before he entered the next chamber, the "Hall of Truth," if his resurrection and divinity were to be guaranteed. Finally, the king arrived in the "House of Gold," the vaulted burial chamber, decorated, like a ceiling in the Ramesseum, with astronomical scenes (Cat. No. 15). Thus, Ramesses the Great had completed his journey through the netherworld and, at the exact moment the sun rose on the eastern horizon of the sky the next day, he entered into blissful eternal life.

Offering bearers brought in Ramesses the Great's funerary equipment, and priests checked to make sure he had all the essentials he would need in the afterlife. As they departed, the last priest to leave swept away all footprints and closed the tomb for eternity. The broom, the remains of the funerary meal and the remnants of the embalming materials were interred beside the tomb, so that they would be available to the king in the netherworld.

Thus, the proper rituals having been observed, the new king, Merneptah, Ramesses the Great's thirteenth son, could take his place as god on earth. The transition of power was peaceful; chaos was averted; Egypt was safe. Once again *Ma'at* was restored.

Servant figures called shawabtis attended to the needs of the king in the afterlife. From the tomb of Ramesses II.

Priests sealed the doors of the tomb at the end of the burial ceremony. From the tomb of Sennedjem at Deir el Medina.

112

Aftermath: Desecration and Loss

Unfortunately all did not happen as Ramesses the Great intended.

Merneptah was in his sixties by the time he became king. Most likely he had gained experience assisting his father during the last decade or so of the aging monarch's life. For the next ten years, Merneptah continued Ramesses II's policies and attempted to maintain Egypt's glory. He erected temples and palaces, commissioned statues, exploited mineral resources and defended the empire against foreign incursions.

For reasons that remain shrouded in mystery, when Merneptah died, his legitimate son disappeared. Instead, Amunmesse, half brother of Merneptah and son of Ramesses II by a minor queen, seized power but ruled only briefly. In the 23 years following Merneptah's death, Egypt saw four different pharaohs. The last ruler of Dynasty XIX was Queen Tausert (Cat. No. 22), wife of King Sety II. Her demise, two years after she came to power, marked the end of Ramesses the Great's direct line. Nevertheless, an additional nine kings of the next dynasty bore his name.

Dynasty XX opened with the two-year reign of a king named Seth-nakht, whose parentage is unknown. His son, Ramesses III, ruled for 32 years, and as the namesake of Ramesses the Great, he made Ramesses II his mentor. Ramesses the Great's ideals became his. He named his children after those of Ramesses II's, and he modeled his funerary temple (Medinet Habu) after the Ramesseum. In spite of these valiant efforts by Ramesses III, accumulating problems began to rob Egypt of her former splendor. He was forced to defend Egypt's borders on three different occasions, and at home he battled a powerful priesthood, bureaucratic incompetence, workers' strikes and a palace plot to murder him.

Royal authority continued its rapid decline through the end of Dynasty XX, until, finally, low Niles, inflation and widespread corruption rendered the last Ramesside kings powerless. It was probably during this period of turmoil, some 100 or so years after Ramesses the Great had been laid to rest, that robbers first violated his tomb. They stole his golden coffins, ritual equipment, provisions for the afterlife and even the jewels on his mummy, leaving behind only his defiled, naked torso.

Fearing wholesale destruction of the necropolis and the consequences it might bring, officials in Western Thebes formed a commission to investigate. They reported that many tombs had, in fact, been plundered. What a furor that must have caused, especially since it involved the bribery of some prominent members of the community! As duly recorded on papyri now in the British Museum, select suspects were rounded up, tried and punished.

The problems continued, however. Several years later, the High Priest of Amun, Herihor, authorized his priesthood to gather the desecrated bodies of Egypt's New Kingdom kings, rewrap them and rebury them in safer hiding places. They adorned Ramesses the Great's mummy with new floral garlands and placed it in a plain wooden coffin which had been made originally for one of his predecessors (perhaps Horemheb or Ramesses I). They laid him to rest in the tomb of his father, Sety I, beside a number of his royal ancestors and descendants. It was the fifteenth day of the Third month of *Peret* in Year 24 of Ramesses XI (ca. 1075 B.C.), as priests recorded on his new coffin.

Still, the country continued to battle with internal problems, split by a priesthood

King of kings, Ozymandias.
Originally, 66 feet tall and 1,000
tons.

which had gained power in Upper Egypt while kings in the Delta ruled Lower Egypt from Tanis. The Age of the Ramessides had come to an end.

Over the next 100 years of rule by Dynasty XXI kings, the tomb robberies continued. When High Priest of Amun, Pinodjem II, died, his fellow priests took steps to end them. Once again, they gathered the royal bodies and used the activities surrounding Pinodjem's burial as a foil to hide all of Egypt's great New Kingdom kings, together with bodies of their own dead, in the narrow pit tomb of Queen Inhapy, which they had enlarged to accommodate the additions. They closed the tomb near Deir el Bahari, on the twentieth day of the Fourth month of *Peret* in Year 10 of King Siamun (ca. 969 B.C.). There, miraculously, for more than 2800 years, all the bodies, including that of Ramesses II, remained lost and forgotten.

Afterlife: Greatness Remembered

His body was desecrated, his tomb lost, but Ramesses the Great lived on. After the monuments of Pi-Ramesses were dismantled and moved to Tanis, the memory of Ramesses the Great traveled with them, and worship of Ramesses the god continued at the new sites and elsewhere. For the next 1000 years, people paid homage to his colossi and venerated him in his temples throughout the land. In the Ptolemaic Period (331-30 B.C.), his cult supported its own priesthood.

When Egypt became a vacationland for ancient Greek and Roman travelers and tourists, their accounts of their journeys, almost without fail, mentioned the still splendid monuments of Ramesses the Great. The Ramesseum, in particular, with its 1000-ton megalith statue excited awe. The chronicler, Diodorus of Sicily, writing about 60 B.C., noted the statue's unbelievable size and quality. Thorough journalist that he was, he provided a translation of the hieroglyphs inscribed on its base: "King of Kings am I, Ozymandias. If anyone would know how great I am...let him surpass one of my works." [32] Ozymandias is the Greek version of the throne name of Ramesses II, *User-Ma'at-Ra*.

The name stuck, and millennia later the English nineteenth century poet, Percy Bysshe Shelley, further immortalized the same statue in his well-known poem, "Ozymandias." By then, however, earthquakes and looting had reduced both the Ramesseum and its statue to a ruin, which Shelley described:

> "...Two vast and trunkless legs of stone
> Stand in the desert. Near them on the sand,
> Half sunk, a shatter'd visage lies...
> 'My name is Ozymandias, king of kings:
> Look on my works, ye Mighty, and despair!'
> Nothing beside remains. Round the decay
> Of that colossal wreck, boundless and bare,
> The lone and level sands stretch far away." [33]

Although despoiled, the Ramesseum was never lost to history. Such was not the case with Abu Simbel, Ramesses II's majestic monument to himself in Nubia, some 175 miles south of Aswan. We know it still dominated the landscape in Dynasty XXVI, when Greek mercenaries marching south carved their names on the leg of one of the colossi. But slowly, over the centuries, the drifting Nubian sands virtually covered this lofty temple.

Belzoni and his men move a bust of Ramesses II from the Ramesseum to the British Museum.

The re-assembly of Abu Simbel at its new site.

It was a Swiss traveler and Arabic scholar, John Lewis Burkhardt, passing by in 1813, who recognized the potential of the sandy mountain and stopped long enough to uncover one of the heads of Ramesses II. Struck by its quality, which he likened to Greek rather than Egyptian art, Burkhardt hastened to share his discovery with his fellow adventurer, the engineer Giambattista Belzoni, who was in Egypt to supervise the removal to London of a large bust of Ramesses II which Egyptian ruler Mohamed Ali was presenting to England's Prince-Regent. Finishing the task in 1817, Belzoni was free to turn his attention to the problem of unearthing the treasures at Abu Simbel.

It was an enormous task to dig down through more than 30 feet of sand just to reach the temple's doorway. Belzoni's workmen, for their labors, earned about a penny a day (and their local chief was promised half of the gold that was thought to be stored inside). Alas, the temple proved to be empty, but thanks to those workmen, the wonders of Abu Simbel became accessible to the world once more.

The face of Ramesses the Great, cut out of the mountain at Abu Simbel.

About half a century later, in 1871, an Egyptian peasant, Mohamed er-Rassoul, and his brothers stumbled onto another treasure which would bring them their fortune and be their undoing. In chambers at the bottom of a chimney-like shaft in the desolate hill between Deir el Bahari and the Valley of the Kings, they found the bodies of Egypt's great New Kingdom pharaohs and the wealth of antiquities that had been buried with them for three millennia. The mummies remained piled, like kindling wood, just as they were when hastily hidden during High Priest Pinodjem's funeral.

For the next ten years, the Rassoul brothers exploited their good fortune, carefully removing choice objects a few at a time and selling them illegally in the markets at nearby Luxor. Authorities soon began to take note of the splendid finds available there, and also of the ever-increasing wealth of the Rassoul family. They investigated and arrested one of the brothers, but he revealed nothing. The mystery was not resolved until the Rassoul brothers quarreled. One of them went to the local police and confessed, in return for immunity, a small payment and the promise of a job as an archaeologist.

On July 6, 1881, officials from the Egyptian Antiquities Organization descended the long narrow shaft of Queen Inhapy's tomb, as the Rassoul family had first done ten years earlier. Aware of the need to work quickly, lest more of the hoard's treasures disappear, they had amassed a work force of some 300 men. Within two days they emptied the tomb. They carried its contents, including the mummy of Ramesses II, to a waiting steamer for transport to the museum in Cairo. As the boat made its way slowly down river, villagers gathered on the banks of the Nile and wailed and pulled their hair, just as their ancestors had done in mourning for Egypt's kings thousands of years before.

In our own century, more than 3000 years after his death, Ramesses the Great still earns universal respect. His monuments still evoke a sense of awe, and the world still pays him homage. In 1960, when the building of the Aswan High Dam threatened to drown Abu Simbel, 90 countries united in an international effort to rescue this most famous monument of Egypt's most famous king. Over a period of eight years, and at a cost of $36,000,000, some 2000 workers cut the temple into more than 1000 numbered and labeled pieces, moved them to higher ground and reassembled the temple a mere 14 months before rising waters would have engulfed it forever.

Today, looking down from his large temple, four 65-foot-high, seated statues of Ramesses II, with wives and children at his feet, dominate the Nile. Ramesses the Great has gained immortality. His greatness lives on.

Head of Ramesses the Great from Abu Simbel.

Colossal statues of Ramesses the Great at Abu Simbel dominate the Nubian landscape once again.

Notes

Chapter I—Ramesses the King

[1] From the dedicatory inscription of Abydos, as translated by D.B. Redford, *Pharaonic King-Lists, Annals and Day Books: A Contribution to the Egyptian Sense of History* (Mississauga, 1986) 265-266.

[2] From Papyrus Anastasi IV, as translated by R. Caminos, *Late-Egyptian Miscellanies* (London, 1954) 150.

[3] From Papyrus Sallier IV, Caminos 334.

[4] From the Kadesh poem and bulletin adapted from R.O. Faulkner, "The Battle of Kadesh" *MDAIK* 16 (1958) 101, 104.

[5] Faulkner 104.

[6] Faulkner 104.

[7] From the abridged version of the first Hittite marriage stela, as translated by A.R. Schulman, "Diplomatic Marriage in the Egyptian New Kingdom," *JNES* 38 (1979) 186, note 41.

[8] Schulman 186.

Chapter II—Egypt in the Ramesside Age

[9] From the "Blessings of Ptah" at Abu Simbel, adapted from J.H. Breasted, *Ancient Records of Egypt III* (Chicago, 1906) 81.

[10] As translated by M. Abd el-Razik, "The Dedicatory and Building Texts of Ramesses II in Luxor Temple II: Interpretation," *JEA* 61 (1975):125.

[11] As translated by D.B. Redford, "The Earliest Years of Ramesses II, and the Building of the Ramesside Court at Luxor," *JEA* 57 (1971):114.

[12] Redford 114.

[13] From a stela of Sety I from Aswan, Breasted 88.

[14] From the Manshiyet es-Sadr stela, Redford 112.

[15] From the Manshiyet es-Sadr stela, as translated by E. Uphill, "Pithom and Raamses," *JNES* 28 (1969):33.

[16] Uphill 33.

[17] From an inscription on the Luxor temple, Redford 114.

[18] From the Manshiyet es-Sadr stela, as translated by A. Hamada, "Stela from Manshiyet es-Sadr," *ASAE* 38 (1938):228.

[19] From the Quban stela, Breasted 120-121.

[20] Breasted 120-121.

[21] From Papyrus Anastasi IV, Caminos 169.

[22] Caminos 169.

[23] Caminos 169.

[24] Caminos 169.

[25] From Papyrus Anastasi V, Caminos 273-274.

[26] From Papyrus Anastasi V, Caminos 247.

[27] From Papyrus Lansing, Caminos 412-413.

[28] Caminos 412-413.

[29] From Papyrus Anastasi III, Caminos 83.

[30] From Papyrus Anastasi II, Caminos 51.

[31] From Papyrus Anastasi V, Caminos 247.

Chapter III—Quest for Immortality

[32] *Diodorus of Sicily I*, trans. C.H. Oldfather (Cambridge, 1968) 169. Diodorus was citing the third century B.C. historian Hecataeus of Abdera.

[33] Percy Bysshe Shelley, "Ozymandias," from *The New Oxford Book of English Verse*, ed. Helen Gardner (New York and Oxford, 1972) 580.

Ramesses II's thirteenth son, Merneptah, assumed the throne upon his father's death. From Thebes.

123

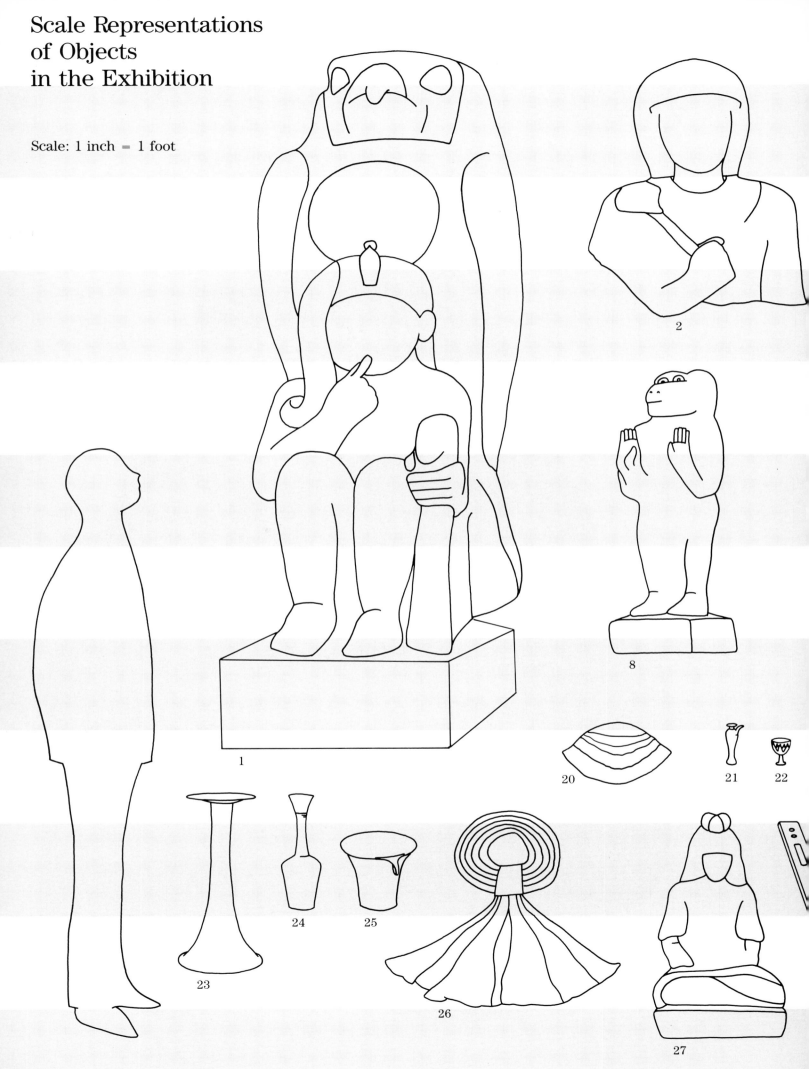

Scale Representations
of Objects
in the Exhibition

Scale: 1 inch = 1 foot

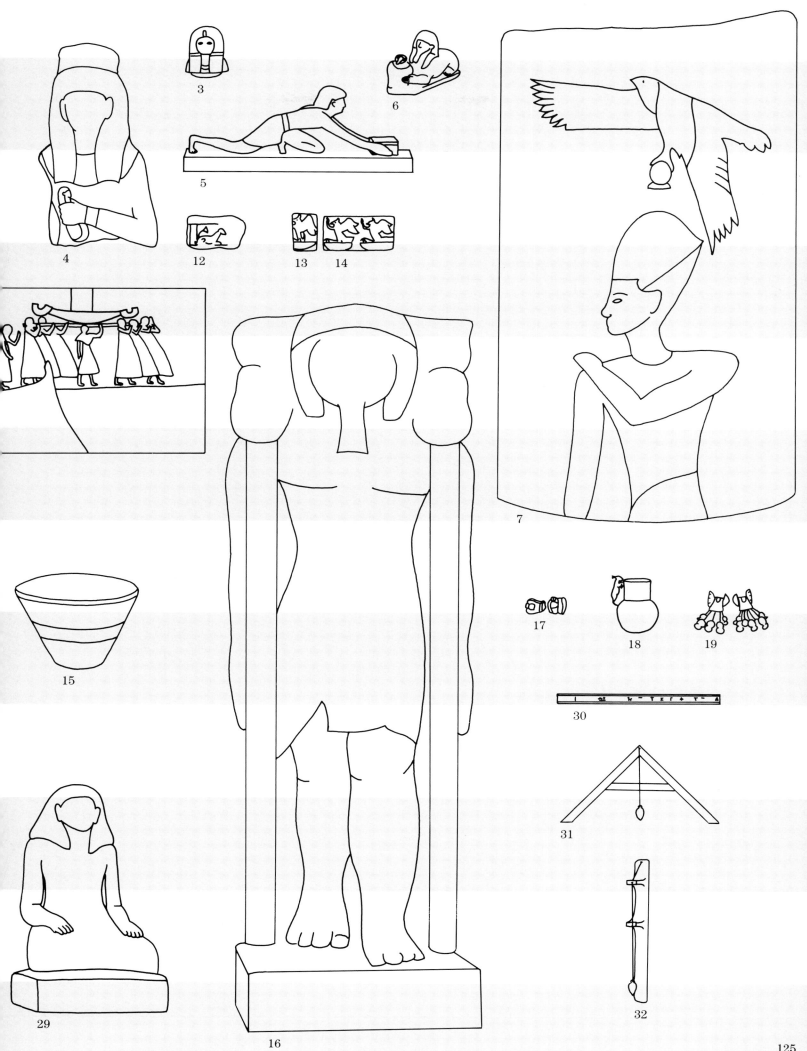

3

5

6

4

12

13 14

7

15

17

18

19

30

31

16

29

32

125

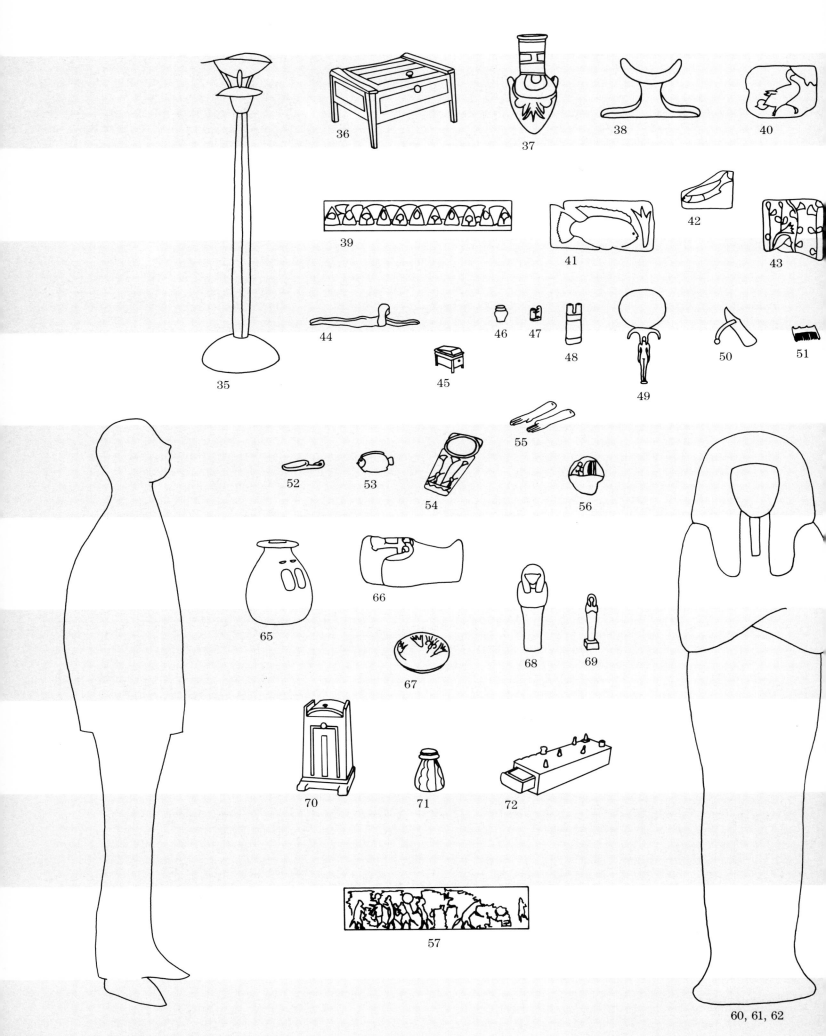

36

37

38

40

39

41

42

43

35

44

46

47

48

49

50

51

45

55

52

53

54

56

65

66

67

68

69

70

71

72

57

60, 61, 62

126

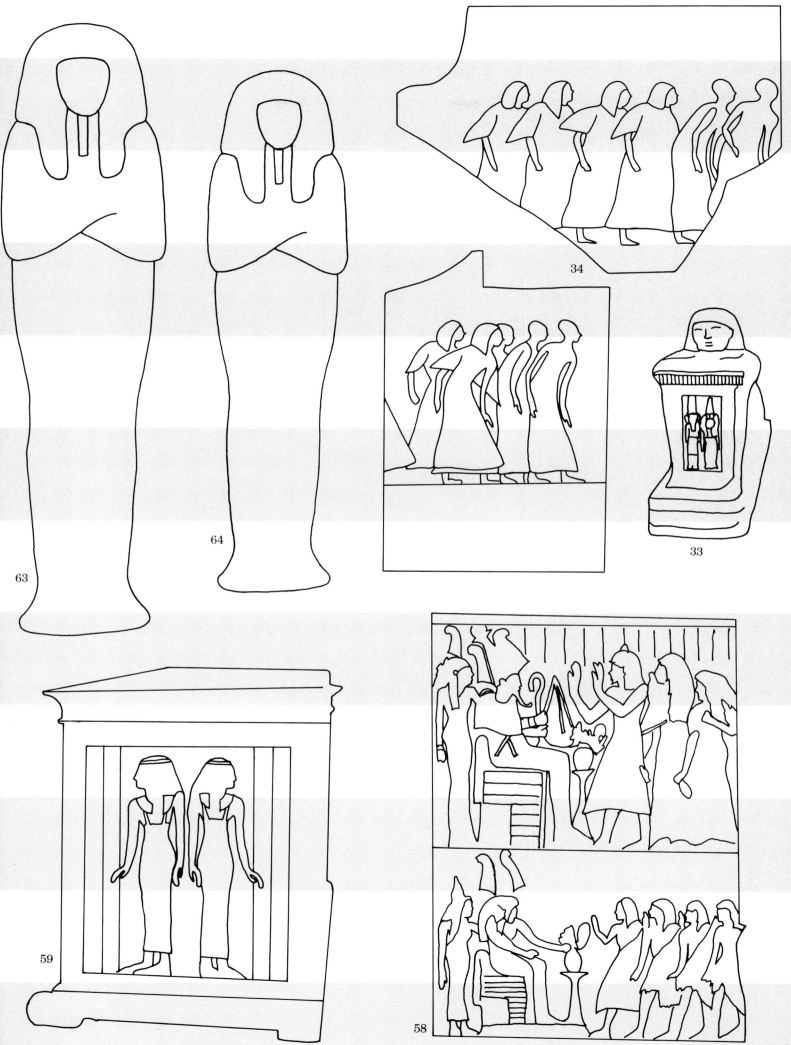

63

64

34

33

59

58

127

Catalogue of
the Exhibition

1
Ramesses as a Child and the God Hauron

The child Ramesses squats under the towering figure of the Semitic deity Hauron represented as the Egyptian falcon god Horus. Whether royal or plebian, male or female, ancient Egyptian children, like the young Ramesses, frequently gathered their hair to one side in a "side-lock," touched a finger to their mouth, and wore no clothes. Here Ramesses wears only a sun disk and uraeus (royal cobra whose job was to shelter and protect the king) on his head. In his left hand he clutches a plant symbolic of Upper Egypt, namely the Nile Valley. Ornamental but meaningful as well, the composition puns the name Ramesses: the sun disk represents the sun god Ra; the child with his finger at his mouth is the hieroglyphic word *mes;* and the plant is the *swt*-plant.

Many foreign gods became assimilated into the Egyptian pantheon in the New Kingdom, especially during Ramesses the Great's reign. Hauron, whose homeland cult centered at Beit Horon near Jerusalem, came to Egypt at least as early as the reign of Amunhotep II (1427-1396 B.C.), when he was identified with the sphinx and worshiped in a chapel at Giza. Both Tutankhamun and Ramesses II added to this structure.

Awesome and majestic, this granite statue remained an object of reverence generations after the death of Ramesses II. It was found inside a mudbrick chapel built in the Late Period (730-30 B.C.) within the temple enclosure of King Psusennes I (1054-1004 B.C.) at Tanis. Anciently, the falcon's face was restored in limestone. It was found in another room of the Late Period chapel.

The inscription encircling the base lists the names and titles of Ramesses and describes him as "Beloved of Hauron."

Material: Granite and limestone
Provenance: Tanis
Height: 231 cm. (90.9 in.)
Base Length: 130 cm. (51.2 in.)
Base Width: 64.5 cm. (25.4 in.)
Date: New Kingdom, Dynasty XIX, Ramesses II
Cairo Accession No.: JE 64735
Catalogue References:
  Brigham Young University No. 7
  Montreal and Vancouver No. 4

2
King Ramesses II

Only the upper part of this royal statue is preserved, and the fragmentary inscription on the back pillar does not include the owner's name. However, the distinctive style leaves little doubt that it represents Ramesses the Great. His round face, high cheekbones, slightly bulging almond-shaped eyes, and sweet smiling mouth are reminiscent of other statues of the king and his family members (Cat. Nos. 3-7). It shares a timeless, forever youthful quality with some of the best Ramesside statuary.

Ramesses II wears a short curled wig with a central uraeus attached by means of a band tied at the back and terminating at each side in another uraeus. His torso is clothed in a finely pleated linen garment knotted just below the right breast, a beaded broad collar, and a bracelet shaped like an *udjat* eye. Combining a human eye with the facial markings of the falcon god Horus, the *udjat* symbolized health and prosperity. The outline of a *heka* scepter, a shepherd's crook which represented kingship, may still be seen in the king's right hand. The torso's slightly forward angle suggests that it originally came from a seated statue.

Material: Granite
Provenance: Tanis
Height: 82.5 cm. (32.5 in.)
Width: 64 cm. (25.2 in.)
Date: New Kingdom, Dynasty XIX, Ramesses II
Cairo Accession No.: CG 616
Catalogue References:
  Brigham Young University No. 54
  Montreal and Vancouver No. 67

3
Canopic Lid of
Queen Tuya, Mother
of Ramesses II

Females carried the royal blood line in ancient Egypt, and every New Kingdom king regarded himself as the offspring of his earthly mother and heavenly father Amun. Accordingly, queens, and especially queen mothers, enjoyed special reverence. Queen Tuya, Great Royal Wife of Sety I and mother of Ramesses II, was honored by both husband and son with statues, temples, and a tomb. She lived until at least the twenty-second year of her son's rule.

Queen Tuya's likeness forms the lid of one of four canopic jars from her tomb. Inside these jars were her internal organs, removed from her body at the time of mummification and specially treated. In 1972, a joint Egyptian-French expedition discovered Tuya's tomb in the Valley of the Queens.

Idealizing rather than portrait-like, the queen's face smiles sweetly from beneath a heavy, curled wig. A vulture cap, atop the wig, symbolizes her royal status. The eyes were once inlaid, probably with glass.

Material: Alabaster
Provenance: Thebes, Valley of the Queens, tomb of Queen Tuya (No. 80)
Height: 17 cm. (6.7 in.)
Diam. of head: 15 cm. (5.9 in.)
Date: New Kingdom, Dynasty XIX, Ramesses II
Luxor Museum Entry No.: J 191
Catalogue References:
Brigham Young University No. 56
Montreal and Vancouver No. 5

4
Meryetamun, Daughter and Wife of Ramesses II

An artistic masterwork of the Nineteenth Dynasty, this royal female statue, discovered in 1896, was long thought to represent Meryetamun, but proof was not forthcoming until just a few years ago. Workers excavated a trench prior to building a school in the upper Egyptian city of Akhmim in 1981. They discovered a colossal statue strikingly similar to the present example in physiognomy, dress, accoutrements, and cultic titles. Inscribed on the back of the Akhmim statue was the name of its owner, Meryetamun, daughter and later wife of Ramesses the Great. Undoubtedly, it is she who is represented here as well. Her soft round face, slightly protruding eyes highlighted by incised lines, and full sensuous lips characterize the best of Ramesside art.

Meryetamun wears a crown of uraeii and sun disks known as a *modius*. Two additional uraeii attached with a band to the front of her long, ornately curled wig wear the crowns of Upper and Lower Egypt and further indicate her royal status. Ball earrings, a broad collar largely made up of beads in the shape of *nefer* signs (the hieroglyphic word for beauty), and a wide bracelet adorn her. In her left hand she clutches a *menat* (ceremonial necklace and counterweight) bearing the head of Hathor attached to strings of beads.

Hathor was the goddess of love, music and dance, and *menats* were frequently carried by women who served as her priestesses, as Meryetamun was. The hieroglyphic inscription on her back further relates that she was Sistrum Player for the Goddess Mut (associated with Hathor) and Dancer for the God Horus. Just as the king officiated as high priest, so too did royal wives have a role in Egyptian religious practices.

Material: Limestone
Provenance: Thebes, northwest of the Ramesseum
Height: 75 cm. (29.5 in.)
Width: 44 cm. (17.3 in.)
Date: New Kingdom, Dynasty XIX, Ramesses II
Cairo Accession No.: JE 31413 = CG 600
Catalogue References:
  Brigham Young University No. 66
  Montreal and Vancouver No. 28

5
Ramesses II Making an Offering

On a base covered with the incised leaves of the *ished* tree, Ramesses II, outstretched, presents an altar-shaped box to his god. At the front, food offerings cover a mat.

The *ished*, or persea tree, grew in the temple courtyard of the sacred city of Heliopolis since the beginning of time. On every coronation day the king's titulary was proclaimed throughout the land. The goddess of writing, Seshat, or her delegate inscribed the name

on the leaves of the *ished*. This assured the king a long and prosperous rule. Here the name inscribed on the leaves is *User-Ma'at-Ra*, Ramesses II's coronation name. Probably this statue was either made at the time of the coronation or later in commemoration of it. The text around the statue's base promises that "his (Ramesses II's) achievements are confirmed hundreds of thousands of times on the leaves of the sacred *ished* tree."

Ramesses II wears the *nemes*, a headcloth reserved for kings, and a uraeus emerges from his brow. Around his waist, a decorated belt holds a finely pleated linen kilt in place. His downcast eyes and reverent expression complement his prostrate stance.

This statue was one of almost a thousand stone sculptures (Cat. Nos. 6, 15, 27 and 33) deposited in a fourteen meter-deep pit in front of the Seventh Pylon

in the temple of Karnak (Karnak cachette) during a "housecleaning" effort of the early Ptolemaic Era (ca. 300-250 B.C.).

Material: Schist
Provenance: Thebes, Karnak
Height: 27.5 cm. (10.8 in.)
Maximum width (base): 75.8 cm. (29.8 in.)
Length (without restoration): 12.5 cm. (4.9 in.)
Date: New Kingdom, Dynasty XIX, Ramesses II
Cairo Accession No.: JE 37423 = CG 42142
Catalogue References:
Brigham Young University No. 20
Montreal and Vancouver No. 64

6
Ramesses the Great as a Sphinx

Noted for his strength and power, the lion symbolized kingship in ancient Egypt. As early as the Old Kingdom (ca. 2700-2200 B.C.), Egyptian artisans combined the head of the reigning monarch with the body of the king of beasts to create an awesome image.

Here, a rather idealized, reverential representation of the head of Ramesses II joins a taut, powerful leonine body. The *nemes* headcloth and broad collar help mask the transition between anthropomorphic and zoomorphic forms.

The human-handed sphinx statue type began only in the New Kingdom (ca. 1550 B.C.). Here the hands clasp a high-shouldered vase surmounted by a ram's head. The ram was sacred to the god Amun (Cat. No. 12). Pharaoh traditionally offered a vessel of this type to Amun on the Egyptian New Year (mid-July). This coincided with rising floodwaters at Aswan, which brought with them renewed fertility for the land. Accordingly, an actual vessel of this shape, often made of precious metal, contained the first flood waters. It might also hold sacred unguents for presentation to the gods in return for a long and prosperous life.

Inscribed on the front of the vessel are Ramesses II's birth name and coronation name. Like Cat. Nos. 5, 15, 27 and 33, it was found in the cachette of statues at Karnak.

Material: Sandstone
Provenance: Thebes, Karnak
Height: 18 cm. (7.1 in.)
Length: 37 cm. (14.6 in.)
Width: 9 cm. (3.5 in.)
Date: New Kingdom, Dynasty XIX, Ramesses II
Cairo Accession No.: CG 38060 = CG 42146
Catalogue References:
 Brigham Young University No. 19
 Montreal and Vancouver No. 65

7
Column Drum Reinscribed for Ramesses II

In constructing his vast architectural complexes throughout the Delta and Nile Valley, not only did Ramesses the Great quarry new stone, but he also reused his royal ancestors' monuments. King Tuthmosis IV (1425-1417 B.C.) originally erected this channeled column, and his names may still be read on it. However, Ramesses II took it for his own use, and his representation covers far more of the surface area. The king wears the *kheperesh* or warrior crown with a coiled uraeus and two pendant streamers, a beaded necklace, and a royal kilt. In one hand he holds three lotus flowers, symbols of rebirth, and in the other a composite bouquet. The ancient Egyptian word for flowers, *renpeyt,* is similar to *renpey,* to become young, and *renpuwt,* to enjoy many more years. Accordingly, by presenting the gods flowers, he receives in return youth and a long life.

The falcon god Horus, whose talons clutch the *shen-ring* (the hieroglyph meaning "to surround" and "to protect"), hovers above the king. It may also have symbolized rejuvenation. Ramesses II is identified by two of his five names, written in cartouches to the left of his visage. One of these names, the composite *User-Ma'at-Ra Setep-en-Ra,* adopted at his coronation, is also inscribed on his belt.

The practice of reusing older monuments did not stop with Ramesses II. This already twice-used column became part of the foundation of a building erected at the end of the first century A.D. by the Roman emperor Trajan.

Material: Sandstone
Provenance: Elephantine
Height: 162 cm. (63.8 in.)
Diam.: 96 cm. (37.8 in.)
Date: New Kingdom, Dynasties XVIII and XIX, Tuthmosis IV and Ramesses II
Cairo Accession No.: JE 41560
Catalogue References:
Brigham Young University No. 1
Montreal and Vancouver No. 3

8, 9, 10
Sun Sanctuary from
Abu Simbel

The cult of the sun may be traced back to the beginning of Egyptian civilization. Ramesses the Great, like many of his royal ancestors, elevated the sun god Ra-Horakhty to a position of importance. Cut into the rock at the north end of the Great Temple terrace at Abu Simbel was a sanctuary devoted to the worship of the sun. Alternating statues of Ramesses II and Ra-Horakhty stood beside it.

Cliffs border the chapel to the west and north. To the east is a pylon. Normally taking the form of two towers with a gateway between them, here the pylon lacks an opening. Entry into this unroofed chapel was through a door in the terrace and up a short flight of stairs. A sandstone altar cut from the living rock stood inside. Two obelisks flanked its east side.

The sloping sides of the top of the obelisks recalled the pyramidal shape of the *benben* stone and caught the morning sun's first rays. Four baboons perch atop the altar with arms upraised in worship. As the sun rose each morning, the baboons' shrill cry awakened the world to a new day. Behind the altar, an open air shrine housed a scarab beetle surmounted by a sun disk and a single squatting baboon wearing a lunar disk and crescent. The scarab placed on the east side represented the rising sun, newly reborn and rejuvenated on the eastern horizon, as the Egyptians hoped they, too, would be. The baboon on the west symbolized the moon and night. On the outside of the shrine nearest the scarab is a representation of Ramesses II offering to the sun god Ra-Horakhty, and on the side nearest the baboon, the king makes an offering to the moon god Thoth shown in an alternate form, namely an ibis-headed man.

Found in 1909, this is the most complete sun sanctuary of its kind known to date, and its form is unique. One can still imagine the awe inspired by the rising sun as its rays burst through the towers of the false pylon, rose between the upraised paws of the adoring baboons, and illuminated the cult images inside the shrine.

Material: Sandstone
Provenance: Abu Simbel
8
Height of Baboons: 92 cm.
  (36.2 in.) to 99 cm. (39 in.)
Base Lengths: 37 cm. (14.6 in.) to
  43 cm. (16.9 in.)
Base Widths: 26 cm. (10.2 in.) to
  28 cm. (11.02 in.)
9
Height of Seated Baboon: 92 cm.
  (36.2 in.)
Base Width of Seated Baboon:
  33 cm. (12.99 in.)
10
Height of Scarab: 69 cm. (27.2 in.)
Width of Scarab: 43 cm. (16.9 in.)
Date: New Kingdom, Dynasty XIX,
  Ramesses II
Cairo Accession No.: JE 42955
Catalogue References:
  Brigham Young University No. 47
  Montreal and Vancouver No. 2

11
Boat Procession

Egyptian gods routinely resided in their temple homes hidden from public view; however, on special holidays priests brought them outside their sacred compounds. Cult images were available for all to revere, and religion became a participatory event.

Represented here is a scene from a summer holiday known as the "Beautiful Feast of the Valley" when the god Amun-Ra left his home at Karnak temple and travelled across the river on a great barge known as the *Userhet* to visit the royal funerary temples on the West Bank. On land he was transported in a veiled sanctuary placed on a portable boat-shrine. Here, in the upper register, the boat is borne on the shoulders of twenty-four priests and privileged high dignitaries. According to the text, many of the officials who carried the portable barque filled important positions at Deir el Medina, the village of workmen who built the royal tombs. Images of Amun-Ra shown as a ram (Cat. No. 12) decorate both bow and stern. The sacred barque, having just left one temporary resting place and on its way to another, is met by Ramesses II's father, Sety I, who offers burning incense to the divine image. Below, the royal scribe Amunemonet kneels in adoration of the great *Userhet* and recites a prayer in honor of the Great God. A description of the *Userhet* of Ramesses III (1185-1154 B.C.) from the Harris Papyrus hints at the grandeur of this divine barque. Measuring 67 meters in length, it was made of imported Lebanese cedar covered with gold and other precious materials.

All could take part in the Beautiful Feast of the Valley by greeting the god in his journey. By means of an oracle, the god would answer their questions. Villagers marked the celebration's end with banquets held at the tombs of their deceased relatives. Drunkenness was encouraged since it broke down the barriers between the living and the dead. After an evening filled with abundant food, drink, and revelry, they customarily passed the night in the ancestral funerary chapels.

Material: Limestone
Provenance: Thebes, Deir el Medina
Approx. Height: 60 cm. (23.6 in.)
Approx. Width: 80 cm. (31.5 in.)
Date: New Kingdom, Dynasty XIX, Sety I—Ramesses II (Year I)
Cairo Accession No.: JE 43591
Catalogue References:
    Brigham Young University No. 46
    Montreal and Vancouver No. 11

43591

12
Ram of Amun
Ostracon

On account of their strength, power, and salient aspects of their appearance and behavior, certain animals were associated with gods from the beginning of Egyptian religious history. The virility of the ram led to his identification with the god Amun-Ra.

Drawn boldly in black ink and highlighted in red on a scrap of limestone known as an ostracon is a recumbent ram labeled ''Amun-Ra, He Who is at the Head of All the Gods.'' A large bouquet of lotuses, a circular loaf of bread, and a fig face the god. According to the inscription, these offerings were presented to the ram by the Foreman Hay who, by doing so, hoped to place himself in the god's good graces. We know from other sources that Hay supervised the crew of Deir el Medina workmen charged with the building of the royal tombs of Merneptah (son and successor of Ramesses II), Amunmesse, Sety II, Siptah, Tausert, Seth-nakht, and Ramesses III (1213-1154 B.C.). Since papyrus was far more costly, scribes and artisans frequently used ostraca for quick, often humorous sketches, for practice drawings, to record minor business transactions and for simple votive offerings like the present example.

Material: Limestone
Provenance: Thebes, Valley of the
 Kings
Height: 11 cm. (4.3 in.)
Width: 18 cm. (7.1 in.)
Date: New Kingdom, Dynasty XIX
 or XX, Amunmesse-Ramesses III
Cairo Museum Temporary Register
 No.: 23/2/22/1
Catalogue References:
 Brigham Young University No. 42
 Montreal and Vancouver No. 13

13, 14
Rekhyt Bird Tiles

Colorful inlaid and painted faience tiles often orna- mented the floors and walls of New Kingdom palaces and temples. More than just a pleasing group of elements, these tiles make a strong statement about the power of kingship. The birds repre- sented are lapwings *(Vanellus cristabus),* the hieroglyph meaning people *(rekhyt).* Their human arms are raised reverently beside a star. The two hieroglyphic signs together mean worship. The basket upon which they squat signifies all *(neb).* Taken as a whole and repeated as many times as possible to fill the available space, each unit reads "All people worship (the king)." A common motif, it often decorated the bases of walls, thrones, platforms, windows, and statues. Although these tiles came from the funerary temple of Ramesses III at Medinet Habu, even larger examples were found at Ramesses II's capital city, Pi-Ramesses.

Material: Faience and glass paste
Provenance: Thebes, Medinet
  Habu
Larger Tile Length: 23.1 cm.
  (9.1 in.)
Larger Tile Width: 11 cm. (4.3 in.)
Larger Tile Thickness: 2 cm. (.78 in.)
Smaller Tile Length: 7.8 cm.
  (3.1 in.)
Smaller Tile Width: 12 cm.
  (4.7 in.)
Smaller Tile Thickness: 2 cm.
  (.78 in.)
Date: New Kingdom, Dynasty XX,
  Ramesses III
Cairo Accession No.: JE 33968
Cairo Museum Temporary Register
  No.: 5/2/24/7
Catalogue References:
  Brigham Young University No. 17
  Montreal and Vancouver No. 21

15
Water Clock of Amunhotep III

Many temple rituals had to be performed on specific days of the year or at precise times of the day or night. For that reason, an accurate method of recording the passage of time was essential.

Every day had twenty-four hours, twelve day hours and twelve night hours. During the day, the ever-present sun provided a foolproof method of measuring time. For night hours, priestly astronomers developed the water clock, or clepsydra. It operated on the principle of gravity. Water dribbled out a hole in the base at a constant, measurable rate. On this example, tiny columns of circles inside correspond to the water level at the passing of each night hour. Since the length of a day hour and a night hour varied with each month, there are twelve columns of circles, each marked at the top with the appropriate month. Alternating *ankh*-signs and *djed*-pillars, symbols of life and stability respectively, are carved at the bottom of each column.

Scenes on the clepsydra's outer surface, once inlaid with faience and carnelian, relate to the heavens and the passage of time. A vignette featuring King Amunhotep III (1386-1349 B.C.) between the falcon-headed sun god Ra-Horakhty and the ibis-headed god of the moon Thoth (Cat. Nos. 8-10) fills part of the upper two registers. By virtue of its size, it serves as the most important scene. On the remainder of the uppermost register, the king in a barque accompanies the deities of the planets and constellations. Symbols of the ten days of the week and circumpolar stars fill the middle register. Below, the twelve gods and goddesses representing the months receive offerings from the king and give him their blessings of life, prosperity, and health.

This clepsydra was found in fragments in the Karnak cachette (Cat. Nos. 5, 6, 27 and 33). Although it was made for King Amunhotep III of the Eighteenth Dynasty, it may still have been in use in Ramesside times. Also a monumental builder, Amunhotep III was held in high esteem by Ramesses II who frequently copied his works. The astrological motifs of the clepsydra are reproduced on the ceiling of Ramesses II's funerary temple in Western Thebes.

Material: Alabaster, glass paste, and carnelian
Provenance: Thebes, Karnak
Exterior Height: 35 cm. (13.8 in.)
Upper Diam.: 49 cm. (19.3 in.)
Lower Diam.: 27.5 cm. (10.8 in.)
Rim Thickness: 2 cm. (.78 in.)
Date: New Kingdom, Dynasty XVIII, Amunhotep III
Cairo Accession No.: JE 37525
Catalogue References:
  Brigham Young University No. 16
  Montreal and Vancouver No. 8

16
Ramesses II and the Gods of Armant

In many cities Ramesses II dedicated monuments to local gods. Here the king, attired in royal regalia, clutches two standards featuring the god and goddess of Armant, a city just north of Thebes. At his right side is the falcon-headed Montu, a warrior god, and to his left is Montu's consort, Rat-tawy, shown with a human head and wig surmounted by a sun disk and cow horns. In the column of inscription on each staff, Ramesses II relates that he made this statue as a monument to "his father" Montu and "his mother" Rat-tawy. The standard-bearing statue type was especially common during Ramesses II's reign. Placed in front of a temple or inside the first court, in this case at Armant, it would have been available to any passer-by for worship. In that manner it served as an intermediary between god and man.

Every aspect of this statue heralds Ramesses the Great's power and majesty. Over seven feet tall as it is now, a hole on top of the wig indicates that the king once wore a headdress, probably the *atef* crown. With its tall stylized plumes, feathers and a sun disk, the crown could easily have added another three feet. A second base for the statue, still in the courtyard of the Cairo Museum, measures two and one-half feet.

Striding regally forth in the traditional left-foot-forward pose of the Egyptian male figure, the king displays the physique of a trim young man. Chronologically, he was at least in his mid-fifties at the time this statue was commissioned, since the inscription on the base refers to the jubilee festivals he had celebrated. Ramesses II wears the royal uraeus and beard, a beaded collar, and a kilt ornamented with a panther-head apron and pendant uraeii. The panther apron signifies his role as high priest giving service to his god.

Material: Granite
Provenance: Armant
Height: 244 cm. (96.1 in.)
Width: 100 cm. (39.4 in.)
Base: 73 cm. (28.7 in.) x 103 cm. (40.6 in.)
Date: New Kingdom, Dynasty XIX, Ramesses II
Cairo Accession No.: JE 44668
Catalogue References:
   Brigham Young University No. 50
   Montreal and Vancouver No. 1

147

17
Goat Vessel

A masterpiece of crafts-manship, this gold and silver vessel reflects the cosmopol-itan nature of the Egyptian empire in the Ramesside Era. Since its primary metal, silver, was rare in Egypt, it was most likely imported from the Near East. The gold used on the rim and handle was probably mined in Nubia, Egypt's chief source of that material, although the animal handle motif is primarily Near Eastern. In shape, the vessel recalls the pomegranate, an exotic fruit to the Egyptians. It was first brought to Egypt from the Levant in the early Eigh-teenth Dynasty.

In the upper register of the rim's incised decoration, stylized palmettes, a motif borrowed from Near Eastern art, frame scenes of animal combat. Also present is a winged griffin, a mythical creature whose origins may also lie in ancient Mesopotamia or Iran. The register below likewise displays hunting and combat, but it is purely Egyptian in inspiration and has a riverine rather than desert location. Scenes of fishing and bird trapping in the Nile marshes symbolize royal mastery over the country and victory over its enemies.

An incised rectangle on the belly of the vessel depicts the Royal Butler Atum-em-ta-neb, the owner, wearing a tradi-tional long, pleated linen gar-ment and worshipping a for-eign goddess. The inscription expresses Atum-em-ta-neb's (and every Egyptian's) desire to enjoy millions of years of life and power.

Rearing on his hind legs and nipping at the rim of the vessel as if to drink from it is a goat hammered out of sheet gold which forms the handle. Although the goat's body is made out of two halves of metal, fine crafts-manship makes the join prac-tically invisible.

Undoubtedly as much of a treasure to its original owner as it is today, this vessel was part of a group of precious objects found in two caches at Bubastis (modern Zagazig) in 1906, when con-struction workers were build-ing a railroad (see also Cat. Nos. 18, 20 and 22). Two objects in the group were inscribed for Queen Tausert (Cat. No. 22), and it is on that basis that this vessel may be dated.

Material: Gold and silver
Provenance: Bubastis
Height: 16.5 cm. (6.5 in.)
Height of Handle: 9.5 cm. (3.7 in.)
Opening Diam.: 8.9 cm. (3.5 in.)
Date: New Kingdom, Dynasty XIX, Queen Tausert
Cairo Accession No.: JE 39867 = CG 53262
Catalogue References:
Brigham Young University No. 51
Montreal and Vancouver No. 16

Ramesses II's Gold and Lapis Bracelets

Egyptian goldsmiths ranked among the finest in the ancient world, and nowhere is their skill better displayed than in this pair of bracelets which bear the coronation name of Ramesses II. Forming the central element of each is a pair of ducks with recurved heads, the characteristic position for ducks intended as offerings to the gods. A large inlay of lapis lazuli, positioned in the center of the bracelet's widest part, functions as the back of the paired golden birds. The interplay of color between the shiny gold and deep blue highlights each to

best advantage. Highly prized both for its rich color and its rarity, lapis had to be imported from mines in Afghanistan. Most of it was probably traded along the Euphrates River and reached Egypt from there.

The heads and tails of the ducks and the bands of the bracelets are made of high carat gold which ancient craftsmen hammered, soldered, and twisted into shape. Another technique employed here was granulation, a process by which minute gold balls were fused onto a flat gold surface when both were heated to the

proper temperature. Each band of the bracelet was manufactured in two matching semicircles. One side hinged together permanently; the other opened or closed by means of a locking pin. Tomb paintings, statues, and the mummy of King Tutankhamun provide evidence that both men and women often wore the bracelets in multiples.

Construction workers found these splendid jewels at Bubastis together with Cat. Nos. 17, 20 and 22. Either they were made for Ramesses II himself or for a temple statue he com-

missioned.

Since other items in the hoard bore the cartouches of Queen Tausert (Cat. No. 22), these precious objects cannot have been buried prior to her reign (1188-1187 B.C.). Accordingly, Ramesses II's bracelets must have been retained as family heirlooms.

Material: Gold and lapis lazuli
Provenance: Bubastis
Width: 6 cm. (2.4 in.)
Maximum Diam.: 6.5 cm. (2.6 in.)
Date: New Kingdom, Dynasty XIX, Ramesses II
Cairo Accession No.: JE 39873 = CG 52575 and CG 52576
Catalogue References:
    Brigham Young University No. 49
    Montreal and Vancouver No. 23

19
Earrings of King Sety II

Men, as well as women, pierced their ears in ancient Egypt, and by the late New Kingdom they could choose from a variety of earrings, earplugs, and ear studs. These tube-and-boss earrings, which bear the cartouches of King Sety II (1200-1194 B.C.), represent some of the most ornate known. The upper element actually includes two halves, each consisting of a hollow tube attached to a boss, one hemispherical in shape and the other floral. Since one tube is slightly smaller in diameter, they fit neatly and securely together. The middle element is a trapezoidal plaque looped over the bar between the bosses. A rounded area cut out at the top accommodated the earlobe. Dangling from the bottom are seven cornflowers, fashioned, like the rest of the pieces, out of sheet gold.

Found in a small pit, numbered 56, in the Valley of the Kings, these earrings were part of a cache of precious metal jewelry and funerary objects inscribed primarily for Sety II and his wife, Tausert.

A few objects which bore the cartouches of Ramesses II may have been cherished heirlooms of Sety II's great royal ancestor. The ownership of the funerary deposit and why this glittering hoard was deposited in it remains a mystery.

His mummy shows that Ramesses II had pierced ears, as did his father Sety I, and son and successor Merneptah. Frequently, kings of the New Kingdom from late Dynasty XVIII on are represented with pierced ears. Nevertheless, we really have no evidence that adult male rulers (unlike non-royal males) ever wore earrings.

Material: Gold
Provenance: Thebes, Valley of the Kings
Height: 13.5 cm. (5.3 in.)
Length: 5 cm. (1.96 in.)
Date: New Kingdom, Dynasty XIX, Sety II
Cairo Accession No.: JE 39675 = CG 52397 and CG 52398
Catalogue References:
  Brigham Young University No. 53
  Montreal and Vancouver No. 24

20
Gold and
Carnelian Collar

Based on representations in sculpture, relief, and painting, multi-row broad collars were the most common jewelry item in ancient Egypt. Worn at banquets, festivals, and other ceremonial occasions, they also formed part of the funerary equipment.

In the New Kingdom, especially, collars were often composed of interwoven floral elements. For a more permanent version, craftsmen reproduced the leaves, berries, and flowers in faience, a glazed ceramic material (Cat. Nos. 46, 47 and 48) easily made and inexpensively priced. Few, however, could have afforded an example as elegant as this gold and carnelian necklace.

The gold and carnelian pendants represent cornflowers (Cat. No. 19), a common and colorful plant in Egyptian gardens. They are accompanied by gold and carnelian disk beads and tiny gold spacer beads. The present stringing in nineteen rows of alternating bead types is based on contemporary New Kingdom models. At the time of their discovery, they were scattered among other precious objects in one of two caches found at ancient Bubastis (Cat. Nos. 17, 18 and 22), a city in the Delta.

Material: Gold and carnelian
Provenance: Bubastis
Width of Present Mounting: 36 cm.
  (14.2 in.)
Date: New Kingdom
Cairo Accession No.: JE 39875 =
  CG 53184
Catalogue References:
  Brigham Young University No. 64
  Montreal and Vancouver No. 27

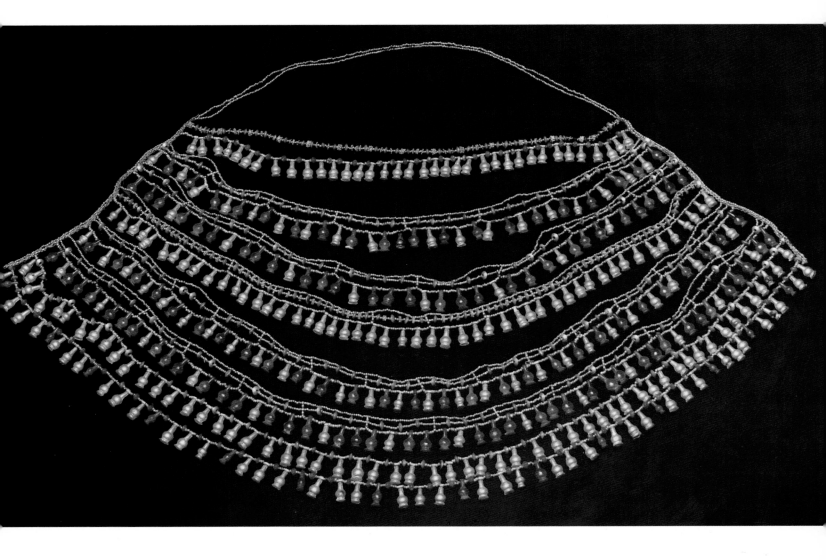

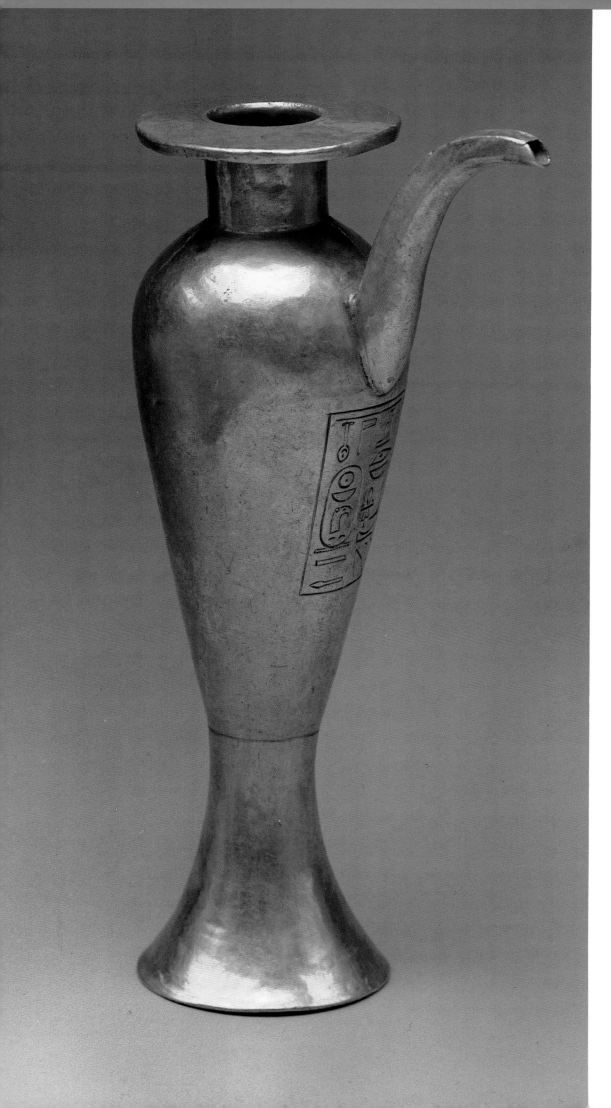

21
Ewer of King Ahmose

Since the gods of ancient Egypt demanded food and drink as well as clothing, shelter, and amusement on a daily basis, the presentation of liquid offerings played an important role in temple ceremonies. Temple walls frequently depict the reigning king in the act of pouring a libation to the resident god from a vessel similar in shape to this example. It also served as a container for the first flood waters and their accompanying hope for fertility and rebirth (Cat. No. 6).

Although this ewer was found in Tanis in the tomb of the Twenty-first Dynasty king Psusennes I (together with other gold and silver vessels; Cat. Nos. 23-26), it bears the name of the first pharaoh of the Eighteenth Dynasty, Ahmose. King Ahmose is credited with expelling foreign rulers known as the Hyksos from the Delta and restoring native rule to Egypt. The inscription calls Ahmose the good god, beloved of Osiris, lord of Abydos. Since Osiris was a funerary god, the vessel may have been made for Ahmose's tomb.

The neck, spout, body and foot of the jar were hammered separately from sheet gold and then soldered together.

Material: Gold
Provenance: Tanis
Height: 14.6 cm. (5.7 in.)
Max. Diam.: 5 cm. (1.96 in.)
Base Diam.: 4 cm. (1.6 in.)
Date: New Kingdom, Dynasty
  XVIII, Ahmose
Cairo Accession No.: JE 85895
Catalogue References:
  Brigham Young University No. 12
  Montreal and Vancouver No. 25

22
Chalice of
Queen Tausert

Skilled artisans have combined the pointed petals of the common blue lotus with the vertical striations of the rarer white lotus on the bowl of this golden drinking vessel. The shape of the vessel's foot and its incised petals recall the umbel of the papyrus plant. Since lotuses flourished in Nile waters and its canals, they became the symbolic flower of the Nile Valley or Upper Egypt. The Delta marshes ideally suited the papyrus plant, which became synonymous with Lower Egypt. Together the two plants signify all Egypt.

Engraved on the foot of the chalice is the cartouche of Queen Tausert, and it is surmounted by a sun disk and double plumes. This was the female crown *par excellence,* popularized by Ramesses II's Great Royal Wife Nefertari and adopted by subsequent Nineteenth Dynasty queens. Little is known about the short reign (two years) of Queen Tausert, the last of Dynasty XIX. After the death of her husbands, Sety II and Siptah, she became the sole ruler of Egypt, the second woman of the New Kingdom (after Hatshepsut) to achieve that distinction.

The cup and foot of the chalice were made separately and soldered together. Like Cat. Nos. 17, 18 and 20, this vessel was part of one of the two Bubastis hoards.

Material: Gold
Provenance: Bubastis
Height: 9.5 cm. (3.7 in.)
Cup Diam.: 8 cm. (3.1 in.)
Base Diam.: 4.3 cm. (1.7 in.)
Date: New Kingdom, Dynasty XIX, Queen Tausert
Cairo Accession No.: JE 39872 = CG 53260
Catalogue References:
Brigham Young University No. 67
Montreal and Vancouver No. 26

23
Offering Dish and Stand of Psusennes I

Not only the king but all who could afford it consecrated offerings to the gods hoping to receive divine favor and a good life in return. Frequently on temple and tomb walls as well as on humble private stelae, one or more gods are seated beside a table piled high with meats, vegetables, fruits, breads, beverages, flowers—all the products of a rich and fertile land. This offering stand resembles the one shown in many of these representations.

The stand itself is a hollow silver tube with a narrow neck and flaring base. Set into it is a slightly concave dish with a deep central depression, intended perhaps for catching liquids. A column of elegantly engraved hieroglyphs on the stand includes the titulary of the king who probably commissioned it, namely Psusennes I, and notes his desire to be in the good graces of Osiris, Master of Eternity, and Wen-nefer, Ruler of the Living. Inside the dish, the king's names are repeated beside an invocation to the Memphite god Ptah-Sokar. Since all the deities mentioned are funerary in character, this offering stand likely formed part of the king's burial equipment. In 1940 a French expedition found these items in the tomb of Psusennes I on top of a bronze brazier which bore the name of his revered ancestor, Ramesses II (see also Cat. Nos. 21 and 24-26).

Material: Silver
Provenance: Tanis
Height: 59.5 cm. (23.4 in.)
Diam. at Base: 8.5 cm. (3.3 in.)
Depth of Dish: 8 cm. (3.1 in.)
Top Diam.: 25.7 cm. (10.1 in.)
Date: Third Intermediate Period, Dynasty XXI, Psusennes I
Cairo Accession No.: JE 86899
Catalogue References:
Brigham Young University No. 18
Montreal and Vancouver No. 29

24, 25
Offering Jar and
Basin of Psusennes I

Cleanliness of the gods
and those who served them
played an important role
in Egyptian religious practices. Daily, priests bathed
in the sacred lake attached
to major temples and used
its waters to wash the gods'
cult statues. For ritual wash-
ing, possibly in connection
with meals, a jar to pour
water and a basin to catch it
were used. Frequently, they
appear together on tomb or
temple walls.

The jar with its squat body, long neck, and papyrus-umbel spout was hammered from a single piece of sheet gold. The basin also was made in one piece with the exception of the handle. For the latter, artisans skillfully bound together bud and flower of the lotus on top, and then underneath, terminated the stem in a stylized palm motif. Three gold rivets bond handle and basin.

The juxtaposition of the papyrus on the jar spout and the lotus of the basin handle recalls the union of Lower (Delta) and Upper (Nile Valley) Egypt respectively, as they do on Cat. No. 22.

Both jar and basin feature the throne name and birth name of Psusennes I, in whose tomb they, like Cat. Nos. 21, 23 and 26 were found.

Material: Gold
Provenance: Tanis
Jar Height: 38 cm. (14.96 in.)
Jar Max. Diam.: 8.9 cm. (3.5 in.)
Basin Height: 17 cm. (6.7 in.)
Basin Diam.: 10.2 cm. (4.01 in.)
Date: Third Intermediate Period, Dynasty XXI, Psusennes I
Cairo Accession Nos.: JE 85892 (jar); JE 85893 (basin)
Catalogue References: Brigham Young University Nos. 14, 15 Montreal and Vancouver Nos. 30, 31

26
Psusennes I's Gold of Valor

Brilliant and massive, this golden collar is the best example of a type represented frequently in the New Kingdom. Known as the *shebyu* or Gold of Valor, it was worn by the king, by a god, or by a fortunate official who received it in return for bravery on the battlefield or a similar act of courage or honor. This example was one of three found on the mummy of King Psusennes I in 1940.

Approximately nineteen pounds (42 kilograms) of gold comprise the necklace as it now exists. Five circlets of flat gold disk beads (approximately 5,000) strung on heavy thread fasten to a lapis lazuli-inlaid gold plaque, which also serves as the clasp. Originally, there were six circlets. Suspended from the plaque are fourteen braided gold chains; each divides into two and then four narrow ropes. Gold floral elements neatly mask each transition and also form the bottom border.

The cartouches of Psusennes I make up the gold plaque's central element of decoration. Divided by a papyrus column, the cartouches are framed by friezes of cobras wearing sun disks. A winged scarab pushing a sun disk, a symbol of dawn and rebirth (Cat. No. 10), crowns this baroque melange.

Material: Gold and lapis lazuli
Provenance: Tanis
Total Height: 64.5 cm. (25.4 in.)
Opening Diam.: 13.5 cm. (5.3 in.)
Chain Length: 30.7 cm. (12.1 in.)
Date: Third Intermediate Period,
    Dynasty XXI, Psusennes I
Cairo Accession No.: JE 85571
Catalogue References:
    Brigham Young University No. 48
    Montreal and Vancouver No. 32

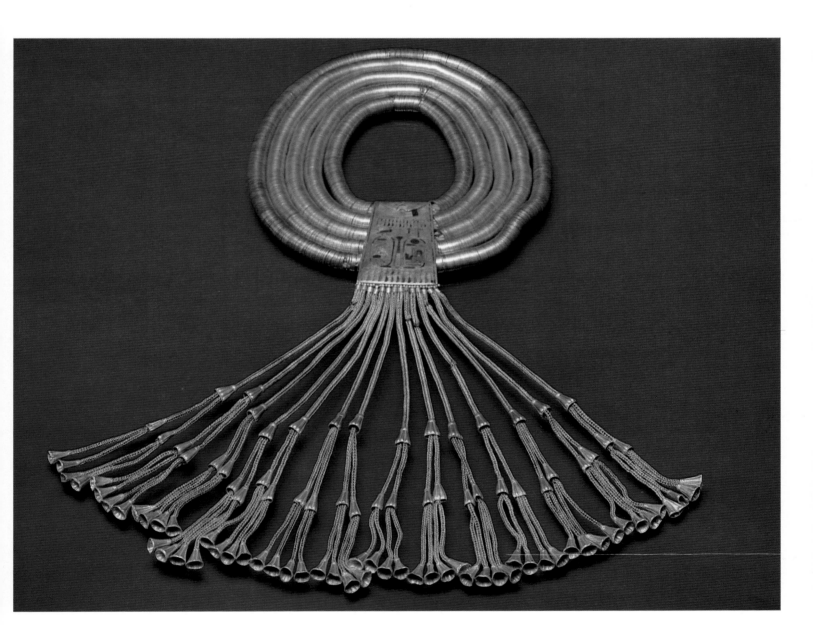

High Priest of Amun, Ramesses-nakht as a Scribe

From the reign of Ramesses IV to at least Year Two of Ramesses IX, Ramesses-nakht served as priest of Amun, a powerful office which carried with it both religious and political power. When his son Nesamun succeeded him in this position, he erected this statue in his father's honor.

Ramesses-nakht sits with his legs crossed under him, a typical scribal pose and a reference to another office he held. The papyrus unrolled on his lap provides details about his life. The baboon embracing his head, offering him both protection and counsel, represents Thoth, god of scribes and of all written things.

Although the high priesthood was certainly the more prestigious position, New Kingdom literary texts refer to the scribal office as the most desirable of all occupations a young Egyptian might pursue. It brought with it pleasant working conditions, special privileges, and the respect of all.

The garment worn by Ramesses-nakht consists of

two elements, both made of fine linen probably pleated by hand. A bag tunic slipped over his head and knotted at the neck covers his chest. A separate piece of material wrapped around his waist forms the skirt. The rolls of fat on his chest and his ample stomach indicate that he chose to be represented in corpulent prosperity. A delicately curled, shoulder-length wig frames his reverent gaze.

Like Cat. Nos. 5, 6, 15 and 33, this statue was part of the Karnak cachette.

Material: Granite
Provenance: Thebes, Karnak
Height: 75 cm. (29.5 in.)
Width: 43 cm. (16.9 in.)
Depth: 39 cm. (15.4 in.)
Date: New Kingdom, Dynasty XX, Ramesses IV-Ramesses IX
Cairo Accession No.: JE 36582 = CG 42162
Catalogue References:
    Brigham Young University No. 4
    Montreal and Vancouver No. 7

28
Scribal Palette

Part of the equipment essential to every scribe (Cat. No. 27) was a palette. In the New Kingdom, the palette was generally rectangular and had depressions on one end for cakes of black and red ink, as well as a central slot to hold fine reed pens. Scribes used black ink, made from carbon mixed with water to make it flow and gum to make it adhere, for the text's main body and also to outline any figural decoration. They inscribed important passages and headings in red ink made from ochre similarly mixed with water and gum. Egyptian scribes wrote on papyrus (Cat. No. 57), limestone ostraca (Cat. Nos. 12 and 56) and wooden tablets, in addition to temples, tombs, and statuary.

The well-equipped scribe would also have owned a mortar and pestle for grinding pigments, a knife for trimming or cutting papyrus, and a burnishing stone for smoothing rough surfaces.

Not only scribes, but every man needed a palette in the afterlife to gain access to the secrets of the god of writing, Thoth (Cat. No. 27), thereby avoiding all the horrible pitfalls of the netherworld. Because the pen slot on this palette is only indicated rather than carved out, it is certain that it was made to be part of the burial equipment and not intended for daily use. A *shen* sign, the hieroglyph meaning "to protect and enclose" (Cat. Nos. 7 and 60) surrounds each ink depression.

Material: Schist
Provenance: Tell el Ruba'a
Length: 32.3 cm. (12.7 in.)
Width: 6 cm. (2.4 in.)
Date: Late Period
Cairo Accession No.: Special Register 305 = CG 69033
Catalogue References:
    Brigham Young University No. 2
    Montreal and Vancouver No. 9

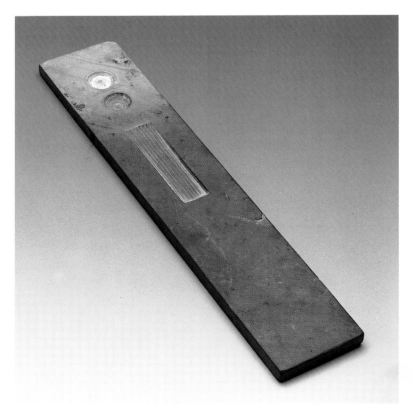

The Architect May

Ramesses the Great commissioned temples and State buildings from the Delta in the North to as far South as Nubia, justly earning his reputation as one of the most prolific builders of all time. The responsibility for executing these myriad building projects fell to his trusted officials. A key person was the chief architect May, shown here in a seated position with his palms upturned in reverence.

Son of the Chief of Works Bakenamun, May followed in his father's footsteps. In his long career, he served not only Ramesses II but also his successor Merneptah, whose cartouches are inscribed on May's shoulders. The statue was found in Memphis near the temple of Merneptah during a clandestine excavation. In 1937 it was recovered for the Cairo Museum.

The majority of the standing monuments in ancient Memphis bear the name of Ramesses II, and May may well have been responsible for erecting them. In the inscription incised on his long wrap-around skirt, he first invokes Ptah, the god of Memphis and patron of craftsmen, asking for life, prosperity, and health. May's jurisdiction extended to other major cities of Ramesses II as well, including Heliopolis, Thebes, and Pi-Ramesses, where he built temples to Ra and Amun as well as to Ptah. He also held military titles. Not only the actual building, but also the obtaining of suitable building materials seems to have been his responsibility. Travelling as far south as Aswan to quarry granite, he recorded his presence in the form of an inscription on the cliff face of the nearby island of Sehel.

A wavy, shoulder-length wig frames May's stern, round face. Somewhat heavier than the ideal body of Egyptian youth, his torso is marked by swollen breasts and fleshy folds, signs of prosperity that come with age. His image evokes dignity, wisdom, and serenity.

Material: Granite
Provenance: Memphis
Height: 74 cm. (29.1 in.)
Base Width: 38.5 cm. (15.2 in.)
Base Depth: 47.3 cm. (18.6 in.)
Date: New Kingdom, Dynasty XIX,
    Ramesses II-Merneptah
Cairo Accession No.: JE 67878
Catalogue References:
    Brigham Young University No. 38
    Montreal and Vancouver No. 6

30
Sennedjem's
Cubit Rod

To calculate land area and to build temples, tombs, and State buildings, the ancient Egyptians used a standard unit of measure known as the royal cubit. Sculpture and relief were also constructed with the aid of a cubit measure, but a slightly smaller cubit was used.

The length of the royal cubit (20.6 inches or 52.5 centimeters) and its subdivisions were based on human body measurements and ratios. One royal cubit represented the distance from the elbow to the tip of the longest finger. It also equaled seven times the width of the palm and twenty-eight finger widths. All these units are marked off on the cubit rod shown here, which belonged to the artisan and Servant in the Place of Truth Sennedjem (Cat. Nos. 31, 32, 37, 58, 60, 61, 66, 68 and 71).

Sennedjem may have used this cubit rod to help build and decorate the tombs of Sety I and Ramesses II in the Valley of the Kings, as well as his own splendid burial place. Although Sennedjem lived, worked, and was buried at Deir el Medina, he, like the architect May (Cat. No. 29), sought the favor of the Memphite god and patron of craftsmen, Ptah, who was revered throughout Egypt.

Material: Wood
Provenance: Thebes, Deir el
    Medina, Tomb of Sennedjem
    (T.T.1)
Length: 52.7 cm. (20.7 in.)
Date: New Kingdom, Dynasty XIX,
    Sety I-Ramesses II
Cairo Accession No.: JE 27211
Catalogue Reference:
    Brigham Young University No. 35

31, 32
Sennedjem's Right Angle and Plumb Level

To ensure that all building surfaces were smooth and perfectly aligned, ancient Egyptian architects and craftsmen employed a right angle and plumb level, both of which remain essential instruments of the carpenter's trade today.

Three slats of wood join in an A-shape to form the right angle, and a limestone bob is suspended by a cord from the top. When placed against a perfectly flat surface, the string of the bob would fall between the two lines incised in the middle of the crosspiece. If the surface were not properly aligned, the bob would then indicate the necessary corrections.

The plumb level, consisting of two short pieces of wood projecting at right angles from a longer slab, operated on a similar principle. A string with attached bob was threaded out the top of the long slab and uppermost short projection. The string would just touch the lowermost projection when the long slab was held against an even, vertical surface.

These tools, like the cubit rod (Cat. No. 30), belonged to the Servant in the Place of Truth Sennedjem who included them in his tomb (together with Cat. Nos. 30, 37, 58, 60, 61, 66, 68 and 71). In the inscription on the right angle, he asks the god Ptah

to ensure him a good burial after attaining a venerable age, and he requests the composite god Ra-Horakhty-Atum to make him a luminous spirit in the sky and a powerful man on earth. The plumb level is inscribed only with his name and another title, Servant of the Master of the Two Lands (i.e. the king).

31
Material: Wood and limestone
Provenance: Thebes, Deir el Medina, Tomb of Sennedjem (T.T.1)
Length of Diagonal: 36.3 cm. (14.3 in.)
Length of Horizontal: 22.2 cm. (8.7 in.)
Height of Bob: 5.3 cm. (2.1 in.)
Date: New Kingdom, Dynasty XIX, Sety I-Ramesses II
Cairo Accession No.: JE 27258
Catalogue References:
    Brigham Young University No. 35
    Montreal and Vancouver No. 37

32
Material: Wood and limestone
Provenance: Thebes, Deir el Medina, Tomb of Sennedjem (T.T.1)
Height of Level: 48.6 cm. (19.1 in.)
Height of Bob: 5 cm. (1.96 in.)
Date: New Kingdom, Dynasty XIX, Sety I-Ramesses II
Cairo Accession No.: JE 27260
Catalogue References:
    Brigham Young University No. 37
    Montreal and Vancouver No. 38

32

31

33
The Vizier Khay

Under the king, the highest government officials were two viziers. One administered internal affairs in Lower Egypt (North) and the other had jurisdiction over Upper Egypt (South). Khay, shown here, served Ramesses the Great as Vizier of the South for about sixteen years, beginning in approximately the thirtieth year of Ramesses II's rule. One of his responsibilities was to arrange jubilee festivals for the king (celebrations of the king's rejuvenation), and he left a record of this important task in the form of rock-cut stelae at the Gebel Silsileh sandstone quarries, some 65 kilometers north of Aswan, where he is shown offering a votive statue to the local goddess Anukis. According to the inscription on the statue in the exhibition, Khay's career also included service to Ramesses II in the capacity of steward and high priest of the goddess of Truth (Ma'at).

Khay is shown in a squatting position, and his body has been abstracted into a cubic form called a "block statue." A type known since early Dynasty XII (approximately 2000 B.C.), it was intended primarily as a temple statue. Here, it incorporates the facade of a naos (shrine) into which are sculpted the chief god of Thebes, Amun, and his consort, Mut. Khay's block statue probably sat in the temple of Karnak for about 1,000 years until it, together with close to one thousand other statues, was deposited in a pit outside the Seventh Pylon at Karnak (Cat. Nos. 5, 6, 15 and 27).

In contrast to the relative plainness of his body, Khay's head shows careful detail. His layered, precisely curled wig, pierced ears, heavy face, high cheekbones, slightly bulging eyes, thin nose, wide nostrils, and fleshy lips are characteristic of some of the finer statuary of the Ramesside Period.

Material: Granite
Provenance: Thebes, Karnak
Height: 73 cm. (28.7 in.)
Date: New Kingdom, Dynasty XIX, Ramesses II
Cairo Accession No.: JE 37406 = CG 42165
Catalogue References:
  Brigham Young University No. 8
  Montreal and Vancouver - (unnumbered)

34
Dignitaries in Procession

High officials of the court hurry forward eagerly, perhaps to attend a ceremony connected with a presentation of the Gold of Valor necklaces shown at the far left and in Cat. No. 26. The reliefs come from an as yet unidentified private tomb in Western Thebes. The style of the carving, the profiles of the figures, and their garments bear the unmistakable stamp of a Ramesside Period artisan.

Set apart on each block by virtue of their spacing and their distinctive clothing are the viziers of the North and South, key officials of the king whose responsibility it was to coordinate the internal affairs of their respective regions (Cat. No. 33). They wear the vizier's traditional long, sheath-like garment held in place by narrow shoulder straps. The first vizier on the block below holds the crook and a single-plumed ceremonial fan. The former was a symbol of rulership, and the latter was a badge of honor frequently carried by high dignitaries. Officials of lesser significance are represented *en masse* behind the viziers. Wearing identical shoulder-length wigs and long, billowy garments, they carry papyrus rolls and walking sticks. The fact that all the officials are barefoot suggests that they were in the company of the king. Ancient Egyptian custom dictated the removal of one's sandals in the presence of superiors.

Material: Sandstone
Provenance: Thebes, Asasif
Maximum Height: 102 cm. (40.2 in.)
Maximum Width: 117 cm. (46.1 in.)
Date: New Kingdom, Dynasty XIX
Cairo Museum Temporary Register No.: 14/6/24/20 = Special Register No. 11775
Catalogue References:
  Brigham Young University No. 9
  Montreal and Vancouver No. 10

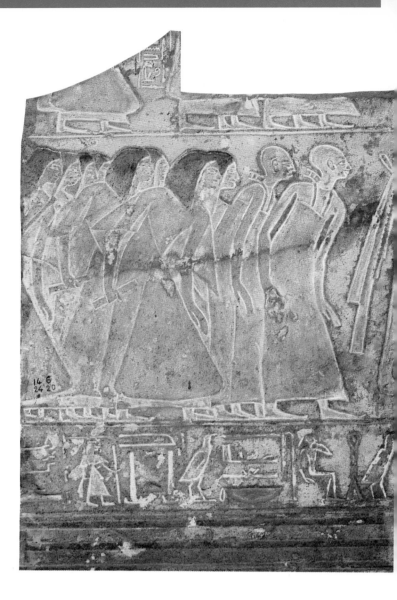

35
Kha's Lamp

To light homes, to illuminate the inner chambers of tombs during construction, and to brighten the passageways of the netherworld, lamps were essential. The lamp from the tomb of Kha, a Dynasty XVIII chief of workmen at Deir el Medina, represents a fairly elaborate example.

A wooden column set into a semi-circular limestone base supports a bronze bowl on three prongs. Fat or sesame oil inside the bowl burned by means of a twisted linen wick to produce light. Salt added to the oil kept the lamp from smoking. A whitish substance (perhaps remnants of fat), charred fragments, a stick, and some material as yet unidentified are preserved inside.

The most common type of lamp consisted of a simple ceramic saucer containing oil or fat, a wick, and salt set into a niche in a house or tomb wall. Here, however, Egyptian artisans have transformed a utilitarian item into a decorative object through the use of plant and animal motifs. The supporting column tapers to resemble the stalk of a papyrus plant, and it terminates in a papyrus umbel. The bowl takes the shape of a fish, with the pointed spout representing a mouth and the handle mimicking a tail.

Records from the village at Deir el Medina indicate that wicks were carefully allocated to tomb workers, with precise records kept of the number consumed each day. Often, workmen manufactured wicks from used clothing and linen provided them by the authorities as one of their auxiliary tasks. Supervisors maintained a watchful eye to ensure that the proper number of wicks were rendered.

Material: Limestone, wood, and copper or bronze lamp
Provenance: Thebes, Deir el Medina, Tomb of Kha (T.T.8)
Total Height: 105 cm. (41.3 in.)
Lamp Height: 7 cm. (2.8 in.)
Lamp Length with Handle: 24.5 cm. (9.6 in.)
Lamp Width: 18.1 cm. (7.1 in.)
Date: New Kingdom, Dynasty XVIII, Tuthmosis IV-Amunhotep III
Cairo Accession No.: JE 38642
Catalogue References:
Brigham Young University No. 31
Montreal and Vancouver No. 39

36
Khabekhnet's Chest

Linen, jewelry, cosmetic articles, and other personal effects were frequently stored in boxes such as this one. Made of pieces of local wood doweled together, it has been painted to appear as if it were fabricated from costly imported woods and ivory, a common trick of crafty Egyptian woodworkers. The lid of the chest pivoted upward from the front to reveal four compartments inside. To fasten it, a cord was wound alternately around the two knobs and then sealed with a lump of wet clay which was probably impressed with its proprietor's stamp.

Two lines of inscription on the lid identify the owners as Khabekhnet, Sennedjem's eldest son (see also Cat. Nos. 58 and 70) and his wife Sahto. The couple resided in Deir el Medina in a house located close to Sennedjem's.

Similarly, Khabekhnet's tomb was near his father's (and other family members), and both shared the same chapel. A number of objects belonging to Khabekhnet, including this box, eight shawabtis (Cat. Nos. 68 and 69) and a shawabti box (Cat. No. 70) were found in Sennedjem's tomb. Like all of the more-than-forty wooden boxes from that tomb, this one was empty at the time of discovery.

Material: Wood and ivory
Provenance: Thebes, Deir el Medina, Tomb of Sennedjem (T.T.1)
Length: 28 cm. (11.02 in.)
Width: 20 cm. (7.9 in.)
Height: 17 cm. (6.7 in.)
Date: New Kingdom, Dynasty XIX, Sety I-Ramesses II
Cairo Accession No.: JE 27292
Catalogue References:
    Brigham Young University No. 34
    Montreal and Vancouver No. 43

37

Sennedjem's Wine Jar

The Ramesside Era represents a highpoint for polychrome painted pottery in Egypt, and nowhere is it better displayed than on this jar found in Sennedjem's tomb. Collars of flower petals separated by framed mandrakes encircle the neck, and a floral garland fills the upper body. From the garland hangs a large blue lotus flanked by lotus buds and pomegranates. Although originally both mandrake and pomegranate were imported from Asia, by the Nineteenth Dynasty they were common fruits in Egyptian gardens. Frequently, the combination of lotus, pomegranate, and mandrake appears in bouquets presented to the gods, to the deceased, or worn at funerary banquets.

The vessel shape, known as an amphora, was common in Dynasties XIX and XX, especially at Deir el Medina. Larger unpainted examples used to store wine were often festooned with actual floral garlands. The tasty drink might then be decanted into a miniature painted version, such as this one, and served to a guest on a festive occasion.

Material: Pottery
Provenance: Thebes, Deir el
  Medina, Tomb of Sennedjem
  (T.T.1)
Height: 33 cm. (12.99 in.)
Date: New Kingdom, Dynasty XIX,
  Sety I-Ramesses II
Cairo Accession No.: JE 27216
Catalogue References:
  Brigham Young University No. 32
  Montreal and Vancouver No. 42

38
Headrest

Representations of headrests in use show that the Egyptians slept on their sides so their cheeks and upper necks rested in the U-shaped area. Perhaps employed more for their protective and rejuvenative connotations than for comfort, headrests were found both in houses and tombs. The semicircular concave shape on a support approximated the hieroglyph for horizon (). With the spherical shape of the head placed in the middle, it brought to mind the image of the morning sun rising between two mountain peaks. Just as the sun was reborn at the start of a new day, so too did the Egyptians hope to survive the dangers of the night and the netherworld and awake rejuvenated, daily and eternally.

The scene carved on the front of the columnar support reinforces the image of protection. Bes, the leonine dwarf god holding knives in both forepaws and hindlegs, leans on the hieroglyph for protection. A snake spews from his mouth. Bes guarded the household and protected women in childbirth. By virtue of his ferocious appearance, and in this example with the knives he holds, he frightened away or destroyed malevolent spirits just as he consumed the writhing serpent. In a similar manner he was thought to guard sleeping souls.

A funerary offering formula incised on the base indicates that this headrest was intended for use in the tomb.

Material: Wood
Provenance: Thebes, Gurna
Height: 20 cm. (7.9 in.)
Width: 14 cm. (5.5 in.)
Length: 36 cm. (14.2 in.)
Date: Second Intermediate Period,
Cairo Accession No.: JE 6269
Catalogue References:
    Brigham Young University No. 40
    Montreal and Vancouver No. 40

39
Floral Frieze

Remains of painted floral bands and garlands suspended blossom-downward from the upper edges of the house and temple walls indicate the most likely use for this brightly colored frieze of floral tile inlays, which once decorated a palace of Ramesses III in the Delta. Grape clusters and poppies alternately fill the spaces between large blue lotus flowers. Inset daisies mark the upper border. Each lotus and fruit cluster was individually made from a mold and then assembled. The daisies and poppies were made from a colored paste inlaid into the designated depressions in the matrix.

Material: Faience and glass paste
Provenance: Tell el Yahudiyah
Height: 7.7 cm. (3.03 in.)
Length: 60 cm. (23.6 in.)
Date: New Kingdom, Dynasty XX, Ramesses III
Cairo Accession No.: JE 21842
Catalogue References:
   Brigham Young University No. 10
   Montreal and Vancouver No. 22

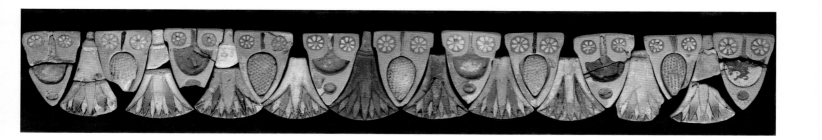

40, 41, 42, 43
Tiles from the Royal Palace

Although the use of glazed ceramic tiles in Egyptian architectural decoration predates the Giza pyramids, no king made more lavish use of them than Ramesses the Great in his palace at Pi-Ramesses. Floors, parts of walls, doorways, windows, and throne daises came alive with color and life. The genre themes represented here probably came from the personal living quarters of the king and his family. More formal and awesome subjects, such as bound captives or heraldic lions, adorned the audience chamber and throne.

The zigzag background of the duck and fish tiles represents water. These may have formed part of a rectangular pool teeming with aquatic life and bordered by low flowering shrubs similar to those represented in Egyptian gardens. In the palace these tiles would have covered a floor, perhaps in one of the rooms of the harem. The sprightly, high-stepping pintail duck with his near impressionistic plummage represents a type of fowl as common today along the Nile as it must have been in the Ramesside Age. Not only was the duck an omnipresent decorative motif in Egyptian art, but also, strangled or trussed, it was a frequent funerary offering or gift to a deity. The fatter of the fish is the *Tilapia nilotica* or bolti fish. Noted for hatching its eggs in its mouth (see Cat. Nos. 53 and 67), it symbolized rebirth. Large bolti fish, as well as mullet, like the one represented in the second fish tile, were tasty foods to

40

the Deir el Medina workmen, who received a portion of their salary in fish. Mullet was also prized for its roe.

On the fourth tile, a woman crowned with an overpowering lotus flower appears to touch a stick to a tall flowering plant, perhaps a hollyhock. Its vertical format suggests it came from the lower half of a wall.

42

Material: Faience
Provenance: Pi-Ramesses (Qantir)
Length: 17.2 cm. (6.8 in.) to 31.5 cm. (12.4 in.)
Width: 13.2 cm. (5.2 in.) to 18.4 cm. (7.2 in.)
Thickness: 2.7 cm. (1.1 in.)
Date: New Kingdom, Dynasty XIX, Ramesses II
Cairo Accession Nos.: JE 89480, 89479, 89484, 89483
Catalogue References:
  Brigham Young University Nos. 11, 6, 5, 63
  Montreal and Vancouver Nos. 17, 18, 19, 20

41

43

175

44
Swimming Girl

A young girl gracefully extended in the attitude of a swimmer once held a container in her out-stretched hands. Judging from similar pieces, the missing container may have taken the form of a duck, gazelle, or fish. The girl is nude except for a few articles of gold-foil jewelry seductively draped over her wood torso. These include bracelets, a broad collar, and bands across her chest. At one time a thin girdle encircled her hips. She wears a short, bobbed wig with a lock of longer hair gathered at the side, a hairstyle common to young girls.

The "swimming girl" belongs to a category of objects not fully understood. Clearly, she projects adolescent vitality. Most likely, the missing container once held a magical unguent whose youth-renewing properties would have been as effective in this world as in the afterlife.

Material: Wood
Provenance: Not known
Length: 34.5 cm. (13.6 in.)
Date: New Kingdom, Dynasty
   XVIII
Cairo Accession No.: JE 5218 =
   CG 45118
Catalogue References:
   Brigham Young University No. 70
   Montreal and Vancouver No. 60

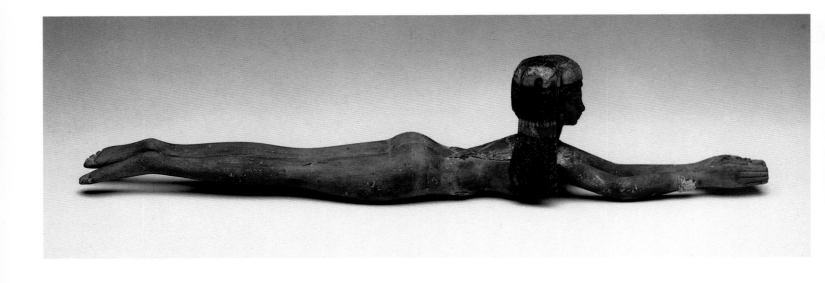

45
Miniature Chest

Jewelry, amulets, cosmetic substances, edibles, and articles whose true significance is lost to us were stored in miniature chests like this example. Made of contrasting colors of wood pegged together and inlaid with bone or ivory, it demonstrates the skill of the Egyptian cabinetmaker even on a small scale. Like many other boxes (Cat. Nos. 36 and 70), it closed by wrapping a cord alternately around knobs on the lid and body. A lump of wet clay sealed the chest.

The sloping lid and projecting cornice approximate the appearance of the symbolic palace of the South, a shape seen on a much larger scale in Khonsu's sarcophagus (Cat. No. 59). The Northern palace, characterized by a vaulted roof and vertical extensions of the side walls, is represented in Khabekhnet's shawabti box (Cat. No. 70).

Material: Wood and bone or ivory
Provenance: Thebes
Height: 7.8 cm. (3.1 in.)
Date: New Kingdom
Cairo Accession No.: JE 3318
Catalogue References:
   Brigham Young University No. 60
   Montreal and Vancouver No. 56

46, 47, 48
Kohl Containers

Both to highlight their eyes
and to protect them from the
sun's bright glare, Egyptian
men and women alike out-
lined their eyes with kohl.
Most commonly made from
galena, a naturally occuring
lead ore, kohl was ground to
a powder and stored in
decorative pots and tubes.
The cosmetic was applied
with a short stick. Three
faience examples are shown
here. (Faience is a powdered
mixture of mainly calcite and
silica which was fired at a
high temperature.) Kohl con-
tainers might also be made of
stone, bone, ivory, glass, pottery, wood, or reed.

Using pots to store kohl
dates back to the Old
Kingdom (ca. 2700-2200 B.C.).
Since the body shape and
color brought to mind the
blue lotus flower, artisans
added its pointed petals in
black glaze. A faience disk
with a tiny projection on the
underside to hold it in place
serves as the lid. Inside is a
cylindrical hollow.

Kohl tubes came into vogue
only in the New Kingdom.
The earliest were simple
hollow reeds. Then the shape
was copied in more perma-
nent materials which were
often fancifully decorated,
as these are. In one example,
a squatting monkey clutches
a kohl tube as if it were a
tree trunk. Since their
playful actions often
mimicked human ones,
monkeys afforded great
amusement, and they may
have been kept as household
pets. Frequently, in the New
Kingdom they appear as
decorative motifs. Two holes
near the top of the tube
were intended to secure
the lid. Monkey and tube

46

were made in one piece from a mold.

The appearance of two reeds bound together is imitated in the double faience tubes, and the vegetation motif continues through into the decoration. One tube undoubtedly held galena; the second may have contained eye paint of another color or a medicinal substance for the cure of eye diseases. A tiny hole between the two tubes once held the applicator. A nude servant girl holding a duck and a lotus bud decorates one side. On the reverse, a similar maiden holds a lotus flower aloft in each hand.

46
Material: Faience
Provenance: Abydos
Height: 4.7 cm. (1.9 in.)
Width: 3.8 cm. (1.5 in.)
Date: Second Intermediate Period
Cairo Accession No.: JE 30776 = CG 3681
Catalogue References:
   Brigham Young University No. 59
   Montreal and Vancouver No. 61

47
Material: Faience
Provenance: Kaw (?)
Height: 5 cm. (1.97 in.)
Date: New Kingdom, Dynasty XVIII
Cairo Accession No.: JE 31244 = CG 3979
Catalogue References:
   Brigham Young University No. 57
   Montreal and Vancouver No. 62

48
Material: Faience
Provenance: Abydos
Height: 13 cm. (5.1 in.)
Date: New Kingdom, Dynasty XVIII
Cairo Accession No.: JE 72178 = CG 3978
Catalogue References:
   Brigham Young University No. 58
   Montreal and Vancouver No. 63

47

48

179

49
Mirror

When polished, this bronze
mirror would reflect an
image almost as well as its
modern counterpart. Like so
many other objects, mirrors
were both used in daily life
and served a symbolic function in the afterlife.

The mirror consists of a
slightly flattened disk with
projecting tang riveted to a
decorative handle. The circular shape was associated
with the sun and its life-
giving and life-renewing properties. The young servant girl
whose nude, columnar body
serves as the mirror's handle
further emphasizes this fertility aspect. From her head
emerges a papyrus umbel.

Other figural mirror
handles of New Kingdom
date feature the head of
Hathor, goddess of love,
music, joy, and inebriation or
Bes, the protector of the
household and of women in
childbirth (Cat. No. 38). Most
common, however, was the
stem and umbel of the
papyrus flower.

When not in use, the mir-
ror would have been stored
either in its own case or with
other cosmetic articles in a
chest. The Egyptian words
for mirror were "see-face"
and "life."

Material: Bronze
Provenance: Saqqara
Height: 30.5 cm. (12 in.)
Date: New Kingdom, Dynasty
   XVIII
Cairo Accession No.: JE 10888 =
   CG 44044
Catalogue References:
   Brigham Young University No. 65
   Montreal and Vancouver No. 53

50
Razor

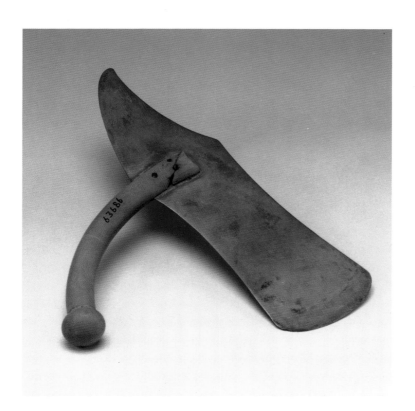

Both for cleanliness and for relief from the heat, Egyptian men and women kept their hair short and wore wigs for festive occasions. Except in rare instances, men were clean-shaven. Flint knives, readily available and cheap, probably served as razors for most. Those who could afford it would have used a bronze cutting implement like the one shown here. Its broad end forms the cutting edge; the wooden projection is the handle. Oil may have been used as a lubricant to make facial shaving less painful. Some barbers served as part of the regular staff of the palace, large estates, and the army. Others travelled from village to village, cutting hair in exchange for food or other commodities.

This razor probably belonged to a woman, one of two buried in the Deir el Medina tomb in which it was found.

Material: Bronze and wood
Provenance: Thebes, Deir el
    Medina (Tomb No. 1388)
Length: 16.6 cm. (6.5 in.)
Date: New Kingdom, Dynasty
    XVIII
Cairo Accession No.: JE 63686
Catalogue References:
    Brigham Young University No. 41
    Montreal and Vancouver No. 54

51
Comb

Fairly sturdy combs like the
present example groomed the
thick, often greased hair of
Egyptian wigs. This basic
form commonly appeared in
the New Kingdom. The ver-
tical shape of the teeth is
echoed in the incised lotus
petals on the handle. Originally, a blue paste filled the
space between the petals.
Combs were frequently found
with other cosmetic articles
in houses and tombs.

Material: Wood
Provenance: Abusir el Melek
Height: 5 cm. (1.97 in.)
Length: 17 cm. (6.7 in.)
Date: New Kingdom, Dynasty
   XVIII
Cairo Accession No.: JE 36233 =
   CG 44316
Catalogue References:
   Brigham Young University No. 68
   Montreal and Vancouver No. 55

52, 53, 54
Containers for Unguent or Incense

Shallow dishes in a rich variety of shapes and materials held such things as rejuvenative creams, unguents and incense. As shown in this sampling, many incorporated plant and animal motifs or parts thereof. The neck and gracefully recurved head of a duck or swan form the handle of a shallow dish in alabaster. Trussed ducks, presented as food offerings to the deceased and to the gods, frequently had their heads in that position. The dish is in the shape of a fresh-water mussel shell, a natural receptacle used to mix and hold cosmetics since Predynastic times (before 3,200 B.C.).

The hollowed out body of the bolti fish becomes the container in the grey schist example. Unlike the previous piece where an abstract shape alone conveys the identity of the forms represented, here specific details are provided. The convex underside is clearly incised with scales, fins, gills, tail, and facial features. The bolti fish was a frequent decorative motif in Egyptian art, in part because of its association with birth and rebirth (Cat. Nos. 41 and 67). A food source in ancient times, it continues to be one today in Egypt.

In the third example, made of wood, the circular bowl is dwarfed by a broad extended handle which also serves as a field for decoration. On it is represented the common theme of boating in the marshes. Two men skillfully propel a light papyrus craft through the water by means of two long poles. A seated calf is their cargo. Incised contiguous triangles at the base represent water, and soaring papyrus flowers and buds provide a marshy backdrop. The combination of the circular bowl, the horizontal papyrus beneath, and the handle's long-stemmed papyrus plants suggest the *ankh* sign, the Egyptian word for "life." The circular shape may also represent the sun rising from the papyrus marshes at the dawn of a new day. In this manner the content's rejuvenative power would have been enhanced by the receptacle's symbolism.

52
Material: Alabaster
Provenance: Saqqara
Length: 14.3 cm. (5.6 in.)
Date: New Kingdom
Cairo Accession No.: JE 30759 = CG 18566
Catalogue References:
  Brigham Young University No. 69
  Montreal and Vancouver No. 58

53
Material: Schist
Provenance: Not known
Length: 11.4 cm. (4.5 in.)
Width: 5.8 cm. (2.3 in.)
Date: New Kingdom
Cairo Accession No.: JE 25226 = CG 18551
Catalogue References:
  Brigham Young University No. 61
  Montreal and Vancouver No. 57

54
Material: Wood
Provenance: Saqqara
Height: 21.5 cm. (8.5 in.)
Diameter: 9 cm. (3.5 in.)
Date: Late Period (?)
Cairo Accession No.: JE 49540
Catalogue References:
  Brigham Young University No. 62
  Montreal and Vancouver No. 59

53

52

54

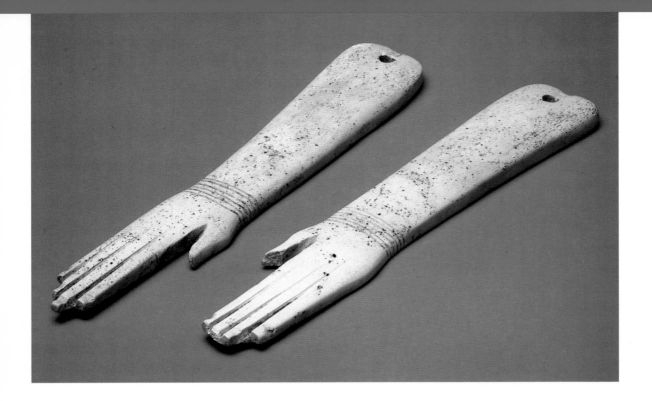

55
Clappers

For ceremonial dances and orchestral performances accompanying banquets, the staccato beating together of clappers supplied rhythm and punctuation. Their armlike form suggests they were inspired by the clapping of hands. Incised lines around the wrists represent bracelets. A cord threaded through holes at the ends kept the clappers together when not in use.

Judging from representations in painting and relief, women and especially young girls most often played clappers. Frequently, other musicians performing on harps, lutes, lyres, and oboes accompanied them. Drums, trumpets, tambourines, and sistra were also played. In fact, early forms of most modern instruments were in use in ancient Egypt, although not necessarily in the same manner. In many instances, the instruments themselves as well as their representations have been found, but time and weather have changed them significantly so we cannot be sure how they sounded.

Music not only delighted an audience but also served an important religious function. Sweet melodic tones could be counted on to soothe an angry god or goddess and also drive away evil spirits. A number of deities, both male and female, were associated with music, and the playing of musical instruments was considered a priestly duty (Cat. No. 4).

Material: Bone or ivory
Provenance: Thebes
Length: 17.5 cm. (6.9 in.)
Date: New Kingdom
Cairo Accession No.: JE 25820 = CG 69211
Catalogue References:
   Brigham Young University No. 44
   Montreal and Vancouver No. 12

56

Harpist Ostracon

A squatting, bald, middle-aged man wearing a long linen garment (see Cat. No. 28) plays the harp in this quick sketch on a scrap of limestone, known as an ostracon (Cat. No. 12). The harp was probably made from wood covered in painted leather. Fourteen alternating black and red pegs on top secured the gut strings, twelve of which are represented. (Harps with as many as sixteen strings were known.) To what notes the strings were tuned, we do not know, since no musical notation has been found in ancient Egypt.

The harper shown here may have been blind. In many representations, harpers clearly lacked sight, perhaps to avoid confronting the gods directly when they played before them. Whether or not harpers actually were blinded is not known.

Harps might be strummed while seated or standing. A different type of harp was balanced on the shoulder. Both men and women played the harp either in orchestras or individually, perhaps accompanying their own voice. Some harper's songs show a philosophical contemplation of the fleeting quality of life and a despair at the chances of achieving immortality; others glorified death and assisted the deceased on his netherworld journey; and yet others advocated living life to its fullest, pursuing one's desires.

Material: Limestone
Provenance: Thebes, Deir el Medina
Height: 13.8 cm. (5.4 in.)
Width: 11 cm. (4.3 in.)
Date: New Kingdom, Dynasty XX
Cairo Accession No.: JE 69409
Catalogue References:
    Brigham Young University No. 43
    Montreal and Vancouver No. 14

57
Satirical Papyrus

Judging from their rich artistic and literary tradition, not only did Egyptians enjoy life, but also they poked fun at it. This papyrus reveals a complete reversal of roles. Animals act in a human capacity, and natural predators become servants to their prey. Here, cats attend mice, and foxes meekly perform menial tasks for a cow. The artist skillfully outlined the design in black and red and painted it with a pastel, almost impressionistic palette. The main figure seems to be a large mouse elegantly dressed and coiffed, seated on the traditional Egyptian birthing stool. A cat in front of her has just handed the mouse a chalice, while behind her a cat hairdresser arranges her wig. A nurse cat tenderly carrying the swaddled baby mouse and a cat with a large fan and a jug follow in procession. Walking in the other direction and totally oblivious to what is happening beside him, a fox carries a jar on a shoulder pole as another pours from a second jug into a basin. Beside it their cow mistress looks on.

Unique in its content but not in its nature, this papyrus belongs to a group of appealing genre scenes, most from the late Ramesside Period, which reflect a topsy-turvy world. Perhaps this forecasted the confusing political situation which heralded the end of the New Kingdom.

Material: Papyrus
Provenance: Not known
Height: 13 cm. (5.1 in.)
Total Length: 55.5 cm. (21.9 in.)
Date: New Kingdom, probably
    Dynasty XX
Cairo Accession No.: JE 31199
Catalogue References:
    Brigham Young University No. 3
    Montreal and Vancouver No. 15

58

Door from the Tomb of Sennedjem

The tomb of the deceased sheltered his body and soul and contained all that was necessary to sustain him in the afterlife. A locked door sealed it off from the secular world. This wooden example comes from the family tomb of Sennedjem, Servant in the Place of Truth, and it is the best preserved tomb door from Deir el Medina. A sliding bolt anchored it to the surrounding limestone frame, and a lump of clay impressed with an image of Anubis, jackal god of the necropolis

(Cat. No. 59), sealed it.

On the outer face, upper register, a painted rectangular panel features Sennedjem, his wife Iyneferty and their daughter Nefer. They worship Osiris, god of fertility and resurrection, and Ma'at, goddess of Truth. Below, seven of Sennedjem's sons adore the composite funerary god Ptah-Sokar-Osiris and the mother goddess Isis. Burial equipment belonging to three of his sons, Khabekhnet, Khonsu, and Ramose, are also included in

the exhibition (Cat. Nos. 36, 59, 69 and 70).

In keeping with ancient Egyptian tradition, Sennedjem and his sons have ruddy skin, reflecting their outdoor occupations. In contrast, his female family members, together with the two goddesses, have a lighter skin tone, since their primary tasks theoretically kept them indoors away from the sun. Osiris' green skin, recalling the color of new vegetation, reflects his role as fertility god.

Sennedjem and his family pose proudly in their finest pleated linen clothes. Normally white, these garments have acquired a yellowish tint, probably from the melting of the scented cone of grease which decorated their wigs.

On the inner face of the door, invisible to the outside world, a sacred game known as senet (see Cat. Nos. 59 and 72) is being played by Sennedjem and his wife against Fate, an invisible opponent. Should they win, their prize would be a blissful existence in the afterlife.

The distinctive palette of red and yellow ochre, aqua, and deep green displayed on the door is repeated inside on Sennedjem's tomb walls and echoed in most of the objects it contained (Cat. Nos. 30-32, 36, 37, 59-61, 66 and 68-71). It bears testimony to Sennedjem's skill as a painter and the high quality work of which the artisans of the time of Ramesses the Great were capable.

The Egyptian Antiquities Service excavated Sennedjem's tomb in 1886, one of precious few unplundered tombs at Thebes. When they re-

moved the door and entered the burial chamber, an amazing sight greeted them. Nine family members in coffins and eleven more bodies wrapped in linen were stretched out on the ground. These represented three generations of Sennedjem's family. They also found household items and tools (Cat. Nos. 30-32, 36 and 37), as weli as objects of exclusively funerary nature (Cat. Nos. 66 and 68-71). Food for a splendid meal—breads, eggs, dates, doum palm nuts, and grains of wheat—was, of course, provided.

Material: Wood
Provenance: Thebes, Deir el Medina, Tomb of Sennedjem (T.T.1)
Height: 135 cm. (53.1 in.)
Width: 78 cm. (30.7 in.)
Date: New Kingdom, Dynasty XIX, Sety I-Ramesses II
Cairo Accession No.: JE 27303
Catalogue References:
    Brigham Young University No. 23
    Montreal and Vancouver No. 45

59
Sarcophagus of Sennedjem's Son Khonsu

Following in his father's footsteps, Khonsu earned a place in the gang of Deir el Medina artisans, and like his father, he may have helped decorate and equip the tomb of Ramesses II. As oldest son, it was his job to prepare Sennedjem's burial. When Khonsu died at between 50 and 60 years of age, he was interred beside Sennedjem and other family members in their splendid tomb at Deir el Medina. His mummified body lay inside nested coffins (similar to Cat. Nos. 60-63) protected by this brilliantly painted sarcophagus. With its sloping lid rounded on one edge, it recalls the shape of the shrine of the vulture goddess of Upper Egypt, Nekhbet, which came to symbolize the Royal House of the South. (For the House of the North, see Cat. No. 70.) A removable sledge on the bottom facilitated its transport from the place of mummification to the tomb.

The brilliantly decorated box may be read like a textbook of the netherworld with funerary scenes illustrating spells from the Book of the Dead and their accompanying texts filling every available area. Isis, Nephthys, Selket, and Neith, four goddesses whose role was to protect the deceased, especially his internal organs, fill the end panels. Their green skin tone reflects their rejuvenative role (Cat. No. 58). Four ibis-headed deities bearing sky symbols frame the end of each side. Two sacred to the South are at the front (head) end; two sacred to the North protect the feet. This prob-

ably corresponded to the orientation of the sarcophagus inside the tomb. The four sons of the god Horus who face the southern, "front" end guarded the deceased's internal organs.

Two registers make up the central panel on each side. On the "east" face, not shown, two genii bearing *ankhs*, the hieroglyph for life, squat in front of a low building. Behind are two Nile gods whose fleshy breasts and protruding bellies symbolize the fertility brought yearly by the flood waters.

Below, Khonsu kneels in adoration beside the mother goddess and mistress of the sky, Hathor, represented as a cow. Beside Hathor, Khonsu, accompanied by his wife Tameket, plays a game of senet (Cat. Nos. 58 and 72).

On the central panel on the "west" face, not shown, Khonsu worships two lions who guard the rising sun. A sign of life hangs between the two horizons, which define the borders of the world. One lion faces Khonsu, the other faces the head of the falcon god Horus rising from the primeval pool of water which originally covered the entire land. Hathor, behind Horus, protects him.

Below, Isis and Nephthys squat at either end of a decorated shrine. Inside, Anubis, the jackal-headed god of mummification, attends the body of Khonsu, stretched out on a lion bed. The five jars beneath probably contained the magical oils and unguents guaranteed to assure Khonsu's rebirth. On the far end, two *bas*,

human-headed birds representing the souls of Khonsu and his wife, perch atop a low building beside a pile of offerings symbolic of renewed life.

Protecting the body of Khonsu from the top of the lid of his sarcophagus are, on one side, two representations of Anubis shown this time as a jackal-like dog squatting on a bier. Anubis' alert watchful pose reflects his role as guardian of the necropolis. On the other side is a figure of the sky goddess Nut. Her winged arms stretch out in readiness to receive Khonsu and welcome him to her abode. Also present are, once again, the four sons of Horus and additional representations of Khonsu and his wife.

Rich in symbolism and representing a highpoint in funerary art, Khonsu's sarcophagus protected his mortal remains from the time of Ramesses the Great until their discovery by the Egyptian Antiquities Service in 1886. The coffins which were placed inside the sarcophagus and the mask which covered his face may be seen in the Metropolitan Museum of Art. Khonsu is also represented in his brother Khabekhnet's tomb.

Material: Wood
Provenance: Thebes, Deir el Medina, Tomb of Sennedjem (T.T.1)
Height: 125 cm. (49.2 in.)
Length including Runner: 262 cm. (103.1 in.)
Width: 98 cm. (38.6 in.)
Date: New Kingdom, Dynasty XIX, Sety I-Ramesses II
Cairo Accession No.: JE 27302
Catalogue References:
   Brigham Young University No. 24
   Montreal and Vancouver No. 48

60
Lid From the Outer Coffin of Sennedjem

The mummified body of the "Servant in the Place of Truth" Sennedjem was placed inside an outer coffin and inner lid of anthropoid shape. These were housed inside a rectangular sarcophagus similar to Khonsu's (Cat. No. 59). Shown here is the stuccoed wooden lid of Sennedjem's outer coffin. He is represented as a mummy with his arms crossed on his chest clasping the *tyet* amulet in one hand and the *djed* pillar in the other. Associated with Isis and Osiris, they symbolize protection and stability, respectively. Crisscrossed columns of inscription on the coffin's surface imitate the pattern of a mummy's outer bandaging. Sennedjem wears an elaborately curled wig, a floral headband, a broad floral collar, and a short false beard. Hands, amulets, face, and beard were made separately and attached to the body of the coffin.

Funerary images decorate the length of the coffin. The winged sky goddess Nut stretches protectively across Sennedjem's chest. Beneath, in mirror images on each side, are representations of the guardian of the necropolis Anubis, kneeling goddesses touching *shen* signs (Cat. Nos. 7 and 28) symbolic of protection and rebirth, and of Sennedjem drinking eternally from the sweet waters provided by the goddess of the sycamore tree. Although all the other images are fairly rigid and stereotyped, this last vignette displays a much freer naturalistic treatment. On one side Sennedjem's wig is black; on the opposite side it is white. Finally, the goddess Nephthys on top of his head and Isis on the soles of his feet serve as divine mourners. They ensure that Sennedjem's body will be protected in its journey through the netherworld.

Material: Wood
Provenance: Thebes, Deir el Medina, Tomb of Sennedjem (T.T.1)
Length: 185 cm. (72.8 in.)
Width: 50 cm. (19.7 in.)
Date: New Kingdom, Dynasty XIX, Sety I-Ramesses II
Cairo Accession No.: JE 27308
Catalogue References: Brigham Young University No. 25 Montreal and Vancouver No. 33

61
Inner Lid from Sennedjem's Coffin

Alert and youthful, Sennedjem's face gazes intently at the outside world from a lid which protected his mummy. Like his outer coffin (Cat. No. 60), it was made from stuccoed, painted, and varnished wood. Of the two, this is the most lifelike. Following contemporary custom, he wears a garment and wig similar to what he would have worn in life. His three-quarter length kilt would have been made from two pieces of finely spun, undyed linen. The first was wrapped around his waist tightly and secured. The second, a long narrow strip with fringed ends, was twisted around his waist and hips and looped underneath to form an apron.

In life Sennedjem's wig would most likely have been made from human hair, with each strand carefully curled and secured to a matrix, perhaps with beeswax. As on his outer coffin, he wears a short beard and a floral and bead collar.

The column of inscription between Sennedjem's feet identifies him as a "Servant in the Place of Truth" in Western Thebes (i.e. a worker at Deir el Medina). Isis, painted at the bottom of his feet, grants Sennedjem her eternal protection.

Material: Wood
Provenance: Thebes, Deir el Medina, Tomb of Sennedjem (T.T.1)
Length: 175 cm. (69.9 in.)
Width: 44.3 cm. (17.4 in.)
Date: New Kingdom, Dynasty XIX, Sety I-Ramesses II
Cairo Accession No.: JE 27308
Catalogue References:
Brigham Young University No. 26
Montreal and Vancouver No. 34

62
Inner Lid from Piay's Coffin

Chief Merchant of the Prince, Piay, is depicted in splendid festival costume on a cover which rested directly atop his wrapped mummy and face mask. Like Sennedjem and his daughter-in-law Isis (named for the goddess), on their corresponding coffin lids (Cat. Nos. 61 and 63), Piay would have worn these garments in life. Only the position of his hands, which reproduce the characteristic pose of the funerary god Osiris, reflect the lid's funerary function. They probably once clasped amulets similar to those held by Sennedjem on his outer coffin (Cat. No. 60). Like the other coffins, it was made from strips of wood pegged together and then stuccoed, painted, and varnished.

Piay's garment consists of a bag-like tunic made from a single piece of linen folded in half, stitched up the sides, and cut in the center to accommodate the head. The sleeves were probably sewn in separately. A second piece of cloth was wrapped around his hips like a sash. The striations on the garment indicate pleats, which were probably put in by hand with the help of a sizing. Piay's wig is delicately curled, and he wears a floral headband. Two narrow beaded collars, bracelets, and armbands complete his stately attire.

Material: Wood
Provenance: Thebes
Length: 179 cm. (70.5 in.)
Width: 43 cm. (16.9 in.)
Date: New Kingdom, Dynasty XIX
Cairo Museum Temporary Register
　No.: 5/12/25/3
Catalogue References:
　Brigham Young University No. 28
　Montreal and Vancouver No. 36

63
Inner Lid from
Isis' Coffin

Isis, possibly another wife of Khabekhnet (Cat. Nos. 36 and 70) and daughter-in-law of Sennedjem, is dressed for eternity in the finest *haute couture* of her day. Here, on the inner lid of her coffin she wears a long garment made from a single large piece of fringed linen. First wrapped around her torso, it was then draped over her shoulders and finally secured with a knot. A large and colorful floral collar covers her entire chest. Rosettes mark her breasts. Framing her face is a long, elaborately curled wig crowned by a wide floral headband.

Jewelry further enhances Isis' beauty. Two pairs of earrings (made from bone or ivory and separately attached), three rings on each of four fingers of her right hand and one on her thumb, bracelets on her wrists, and beaded strands entwined around her arms complete her splendid costume.

In both hands, Isis clasps delicate tendrils of a creeper vine. Found also in association with nude servant girls and birthing stools, this plant probably had a symbolic connection with birth and rejuvenation. On the soles of her feet, her divine namesake, the goddess Isis, holds aloft two *ankh* signs (signifying life) while two *djed* pillars (stability) dangle from the goddess' elbows.

A column of hierogylphs between her feet identifies Isis as the owner of this coffin lid. A single-line inscription around the perimeter invokes a variety of gods.

Material: Wood
Provenance: Thebes, Deir el Medina, Tomb of Sennedjem (T.T.1)
Length: 193 cm. (75.98 in.)
Width: 47 cm. (18.5 in.)
Date: New Kingdom, Dynasty XIX, Sety I-Ramesses II
Cairo Accession No.: JE 27309
Catalogue References:
  Brigham Young University No. 27
  Montreal and Vancouver No. 35

Of all the gold, costly jewels, and other precious equipment that surely accompanied Ramesses II in his tomb, little remains that can be identified with certainty (Cat. No. 65). Although this cedar lid covered his mummy, the soft treatment of the facial features leaves little doubt that it was made for one of Ramesses II's royal predecessors, either in the late Eighteenth or early Nineteenth Dynasty, perhaps for his grandfather, Ramesses I. The wood was imported from Lebanon. A hurriedly inked inscription on the legs and on top of the head records its painful history.

Stripped of all valuables in the two centuries following his death, Ramesses II's desecrated body, together with those of several other prominent kings, was rewrapped and moved to Sety I's tomb by order of the High Priest of Amun, Herihor. This took place in Year Twenty-Four of Ramesses XI (ca. 1075 B.C.), on the Fifteenth day of the Third month of *Peret*. Still vulnerable, it was moved yet again to a safer stronghold in the tomb of Queen Inhapy, just south of Deir el Bahari together with nearly forty other royal mummies. This trip occupied three days in the Fourth month of *Peret* in the Tenth Year of the reign of Siamun (ca. 969 B.C.), from day Seventeen through Twenty. There they remained until their discovery in A.D. 1881.

This coffin lid probably resembles the way one of Ramesses II's coffin lids would have looked stripped of its gold and inlaid precious stone covering. The crossed hands, a characteristic pose of royal mummies, hold the crook and flail of rulership (probably added during one of the reburials). A divine cobra (uraeus) emerges from the front of the royal headcloth *(nemes)* to shelter and protect the king.

Material: Wood
Provenance: Thebes, near Deir el Bahari
Height: 206 cm. (81.1 in.)
Width: 54.5 cm. (21.5 in.)
Depth at Foot: 36.5 cm. (14.4 in.)
Date: Coffin: New Kingdom, Dynasty XVIII or XIX
　Inscriptions: New Kingdom and Third Intermediate Period, Dynasty XX and Dynasty XXI
Cairo Accession No.: JE 26214 = CG 61020
Catalogue References:
　Brigham Young University No. 55
　Montreal and Vancouver No. 66

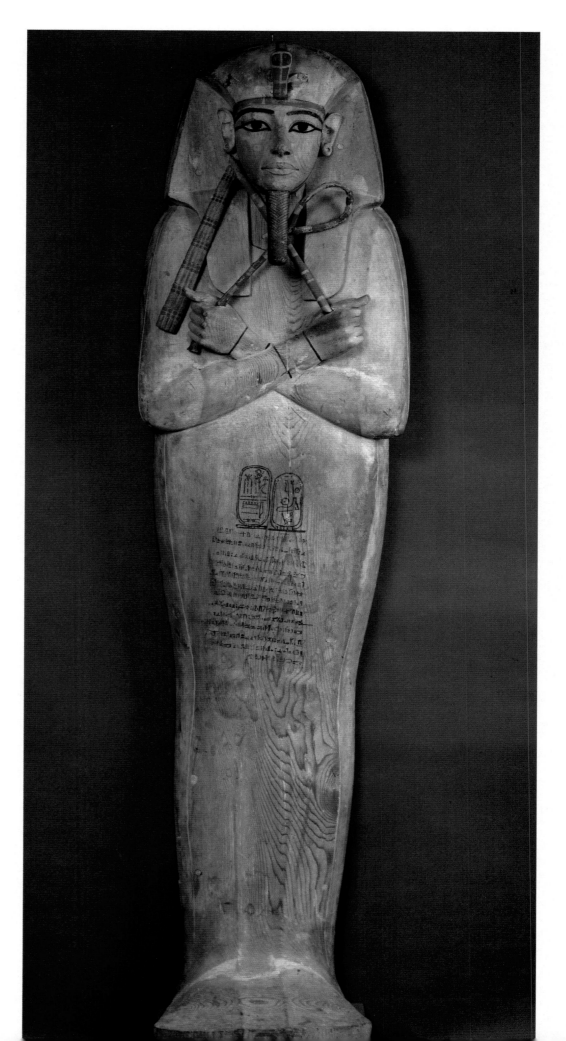

Alabaster Vessel of Ramesses II

Since Ramesses the Great's tomb suffered near-total destruction at the hands of ancient plunderers, nothing remains that can unquestionably be identified as having been buried with the king (Cat. No. 64), except for a few of his shawabtis. However, since this alabaster vessel bears two incised and inlaid cartouches of Ramesses II and since it was found in the Valley of the Kings beside the tomb of Merneptah not far from Ramesses II's tomb, it possibly was part of Ramesses II's original burial equipment. Perhaps plunderers tossed it aside so as not to be burdened by its weight after they had emptied it of its precious contents. Alternatively, it may have contained some of the embalming materials of the king, which were buried together with the remains of his funerary feast following the burial ceremony.

Vessels of this shape, called alabastra, were common in Egypt in Dynasties XVIII and XIX and could be made from clay as well as stone (Cat. No. 71). They were often sealed with simple, disk-shaped lids. An analysis of the contents of similarly shaped vessels indicates that some held scented unguents intended for a cosmetic or ritual purpose.

Material: Alabaster inlaid with
   paste
Provenance: Thebes, Valley of the
   Kings
Height: 26.6 cm. (10.5 in.)
Date: New Kingdom, Dynasty XIX,
   Ramesses II
Cairo Accession No.: JE 46712
Catalogue References:
   Brigham Young University No. 13
   Montreal and Vancouver No. 44

66
Canopic Coffin of Sennedjem

Reproducing in miniature his outermost coffin (Cat. No. 60), this limestone box once protected one of Sennedjem's internal organs. To prevent the body from decaying, embalmers removed most of the viscera through a slit in the left side, and then they covered it with powdered natron to dry it out. The liver, lungs, stomach, and intestines were most often stored in vessels known as canopic jars. Here, in imitation of a royal custom seen in the tomb of Tutankhamun, Sennedjem has substituted a mummiform coffin shape for a jar. One of the four sons of Horus (Cat. No. 59) would have protected each organ.

Sennedjem's linen-wrapped, white body and crossed arms identify him here as a mummy. The bands of inscription across his torso, which imitate the mummy's final wrappings, include Sennedjem's name and titles and invoke the favor of funerary deities. The yellow and blue stripes on his long, heavy wig reproduce in paint what Tutankhamun, and probably other kings as well, rendered in glistening gold and lapis lazuli.

Material: Limestone
Provenance: Thebes, Deir el Medina, Tomb of Sennedjem (T.T.1)
Height: 34 cm. (13.4 in.)
Date: New Kingdom, Dynasty XIX, Sety I-Ramesses II
Cairo Accession No.: Special Register 41 = CG 4251
Catalogue References: Brigham Young University No. 21 Montreal and Vancouver No. 47

67
Faience Bowl

Filled with aquatic motifs painted in black against a blue-glazed background, this bowl belongs to a type common in New Kingdom tombs and temples. It probably contained a rejuvenative liquid refreshment, perhaps milk, wine, or water, intended either for the deceased or for the gods.

Although water, indicated by wavy lines, is shown only in the rectangular pool in the center, the entirety of the bowl's interior represents a pond. Decorative but symbolic as well, the images inside relate to the theme of rebirth. The lotus flowers radiating from each corner of the central rectangle suggest rejuvenation: they close each evening to reopen with the dawning of a new day just as the sun god was reborn every morning. On two sides of the pool, bolti fish *(Tilapia nilotica)* nibble lotus buds. The Egyptians noted that these fish incubate and hatch their eggs inside their mouths. The tiny newborns emerging suggest an image of spontaneous generation and fertility. Associated with the goddess Hathor, they formed a duality with the sun god as represented by the lotus flower. Stylized palmettes occupying the remaining space symbolize the tree of life.

Material: Faience
Provenance: Thebes, Deir el
    Medina (Tomb No. 1382)
Diameter: 17 cm. (6.7 in.)
Date: New Kingdom, Dynasty
    XVIII
Cairo Accession No.: JE 63677
Catalogue References:
    Brigham Young University No. 39
    Montreal and Vancouver No. 41

Shawabtis of Sennedjem and Ramose

While the deceased enjoyed every possible pleasure in the afterlife, miniature servant figures called shawabtis took care of any work that awaited. Sennedjem's shawabti is shown here, as well as one belonging to his son, Ramose. Their poses and attributes are characteristic of shawabtis, namely, they are wrapped as mummies, and their crossed arms clutch agricultural tools (in this case, two hoes). A bag to carry grain is often suspended on the back (Sennedjem's shawabti carries two). A total of nine shawabtis of Sennedjem and three shawabtis of Ramose were found in Sennedjem's family tomb. It was customary later on to provide one shawabti for each day of the year and one supervisor shawabti for every ten workers, a total of 401. Kings included shawabtis in their burial equipment, often in even greater numbers.

Eight lines of inscription encircling Sennedjem's shawabti contain the traditional shawabti prayer excerpted from Chapter Six of the *Book of the Dead:*

> O shawabti! If the Osiris Sennedjem is called upon to do any of the work which a man does in the necropolis, namely to cultivate the fields, to water the banks, to transport sand from the East to the West, "Here I am!" you shall say.

The inscription on Ramose's shawabti contains only his name and his epithet, Child of the Tomb, signifying that his father Sennedjem was part of the gang of Deir el Medina workmen charged with construction of the royal tombs. In all likelihood, he died before he could follow in his father's footsteps. Ramose stands fifth in line on the outside of his family tomb door (Cat. No. 58, lower register).

68
Material: Limestone
Provenance: Thebes, Deir el Medina, Tomb of Sennedjem (T.T.1)
Height: 29 cm. (11.4 in.)
Date: New Kingdom, Dynasty XIX, Sety I-Ramesses II
Cairo Accession No.: JE 27251 = CG 47740
Catalogue References: Brigham Young University No. 30 Montreal and Vancouver No. 52

69
Material: Limestone
Provenance: Thebes, Deir el Medina, Tomb of Sennedjem (T.T.1)
Height: 19 cm. (7.5 in.)
Date: New Kingdom, Dynasty XIX, Sety I-Ramesses II
Cairo Accession No.: JE 27232 = CG 47765
Catalogue References: Brigham Young University No. 29 Montreal and Vancouver No. 51

Khabekhnet's Shawabti Box

In the New Kingdom special care was taken with shawabtis (Cat. Nos. 68-69), and they were often stored in pairs in chests similar in shape to this one. Later, shawabtis were mass-produced and stored by the hundreds in crude, often undecorated wooden boxes. In this splendid example, the vaulted lid, vertical projections, and ''palace facade'' decoration imitate the appearance of the sanctuary of Lower Egypt sacred to the cobra goddess Wadjet, which was often juxtaposed with the holy shrine of Upper Egypt (Cat. Nos. 45 and 59). Together, they brought to mind the duality of the country united under a single divine monarch. The box/shrine rests on runners, which here are strictly ornamental, but on larger items (Cat. No. 59) would have facilitated transport across the sand. One Deir el Medina villager exchanged the equivalent of two deben of copper (182 grams) to obtain a shawabti box, and a record of this transaction was inscribed on an ostracon (Cat. Nos. 12 and 56).

A central column of inscription on each side of the shawabti box identifies its owner, ''The Revered One under Osiris (god of the netherworld) Khabekhnet, justified.'' Khabekhnet, the eldest of Sennedjem's seven sons and one of ten children, is represented on the outside door of his father's family tomb (Cat. No. 58, bottom register, first in line). Many objects belonging to Khabekhnet were found inside, including a painted wooden chest in the exhibition (Cat. No. 36). His own tomb lay next door. Most likely, he was born during the reign of Sety I and was active during Ramesses II's rule.

Material: Wood
Provenance: Thebes, Deir el Medina, Tomb of Sennedjem (T.T.1)
Height: 30 cm. (11.8 in.)
Date: New Kingdom, Dynasty XIX, Sety I-Ramesses II
Cairo Accession No.: JE 27296
Catalogue References:
    Brigham Young University No. 22
    Montreal and Vancouver No. 50

Sennedjem's Imitation Stone Vessel

Artisans of the New Kingdom mastered the art of clever copying, a technique practiced almost since the beginning of recorded history in Egypt. Precious stones were imitated in glass and faience; cheap local woods were veneered in imported ebony and ivory; and pottery was painted to look like stone. Here, a simple buff-colored ceramic vessel resembles veined alabaster through the addition of white paint and multi-colored wavy lines. A ceramic disk painted with an abstract floral design forms the lid. The inscription identifies Sennedjem as the vessel's owner.

The bag-like shape, called an alabastron, is typically Egyptian and seems, in some instances, to have contained scented fat (Cat. No. 65). In the New Kingdom many examples were manufactured in stone and faience as well as pottery. Through trade, some found their way to the Aegean world where they were copied in local materials.

Material: Pottery
Provenance: Thebes, Deir el Medina, Tomb of Sennedjem (T.T.1)
Height: 14.5 cm. (5.7 in.)
Date: New Kingdom, Dynasty XIX, Sety I-Ramesses II
Cairo Accession No.: JE 27248
Catalogue References:
    Brigham Young University No. 36
    Montreal and Vancouver No. 49

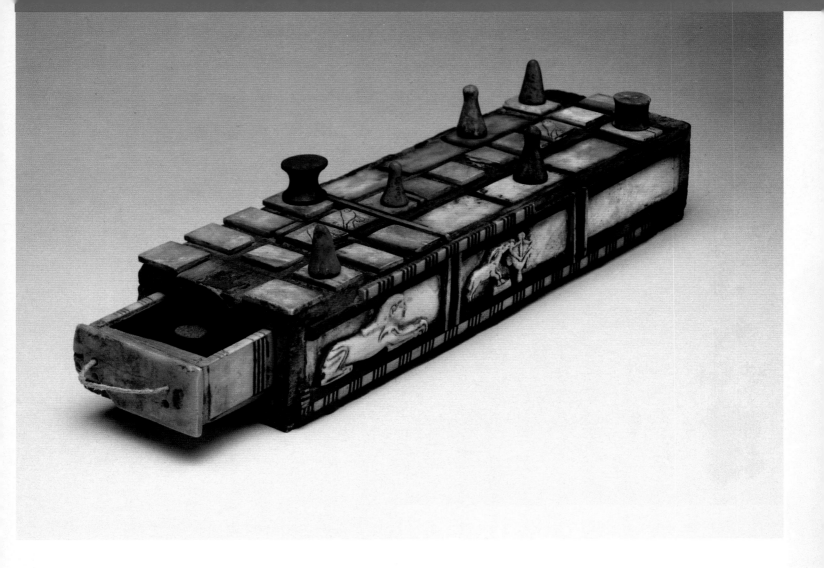

72
Senet Game

Since the beginning of their recorded history (ca. 3200 B.C.), the Egyptians displayed a fondness for board games. They played them both for personal amusement and for their religious significance. Of all the board games, senet, shown here, achieved the greatest popularity.

Two opponents played the game, and each had his own distinctive playing pieces (between five and ten per player). The object was to move those pieces across the thirty squares (three rows of ten) of the game board. The throw of a knucklebone or the tossing of a set of throwsticks determined the number of squares moved. It was considered fortunate to land on some squares, while others brought bad luck, such as being forced to return to the start. The first player to move all his pieces off the board won the game.

Especially during the Ramesside Era, playing senet was rich in symbolism. One played not with an earthly partner but against Fate himself, and moving one's pieces across the game board was synonymous with traversing the pitfalls of the netherworld. Eternal life was the prize for victory. Both Sennedjem and Khonsu are shown playing senet against an invisible other-worldly opponent on their tomb door (Cat. No. 58) and sarcophagus (Cat. No. 59) respectively.

The drawer inside this ebony and ivory inlaid board stored the playing pieces. A sphinx and an ibex nibbling from the tree of life decorate the side panels.

Material: Box: Bone and ebony
  Game Pieces: Faience
Provenance: Thebes, Dra Abu'l
  Naga
Length: 26 cm. (10.2 in.)
Width: 7.6 cm. (2.99 in.)
Height: 4.7 cm. (1.9 in.)
Date: Second Intermediate Period,
  Dynasty XVII
Cairo Accession No.: JE 21462
Catalogue References:
  Brigham Young University No. 52
  Montreal and Vancouver No. 46

Suggestions for Further Reading

General

Aldred, C. *Egyptian Art* (New York and Toronto, 1980).

Baines, J., and Málek, J. *Atlas of Ancient Egypt* (New York, 1980).

Desroches-Noblecourt, C. *The Great Pharaoh Ramses II and his Time.* An exhibition of antiquities from the Egyptian Museum, Cairo. Palais de la Civilisation, Montréal. June 1-September 29, 1985 (Montreal, 1985).

Edwards, I. E. S. et al., eds. *Cambridge Ancient History, I-III* rev. ed. (Cambridge, 1970-82).

Harris, J. R., ed. *The Legacy of Egypt* (Oxford, 1971).

Hayes, W. C. *The Scepter of Egypt, Part II* (New York, 1959).

James, T. G. H. *An Introduction to Ancient Egypt* (London, 1979).

Kees, H. *Ancient Egypt* (Chicago, 1961).

Mertz, B. *Red Land, Black Land* (New York, 1966).

Sabbahy, L. *Ramses II: The Pharaoh and His Time.* Exhibition Catalog. Brigham Young University. 25 October 1985 to 5 April 1986 (Provo, 1985).

Smith, W. S. *The Art and Architecture of Ancient Egypt* rev. ed. by W. K. Simpson (New York, 1981).

Chapter I—Ramesses the King

Bietak, M. *Avaris and Piramesse: Archaeological Exploration in the Eastern Nile Delta* (London, 1981).

Dimick, M. T. *Memphis, The City of the White Wall* (Philadelphia, 1956).

Gaballa, A. *Narrative in Egyptian Art* (Mainz, 1976).

Gardiner, A. *The Kadesh Inscriptions of Ramesses II* (Oxford, 1960).

Goedicke, H., ed. *Perspectives on the Battle of Kadesh* (Baltimore, 1985).

Hayes, W. C. *Glazed Tiles from a Palace of Ramesses II at Kantir.* 1937 (New York, 1973).

Jeffreys, D. G. *The Survey of Memphis I* (London, 1985).

Kitchen, K. A. *Pharaoh Triumphant: The Life and Times of Ramesses II* (Mississauga, Canada, 1982).

Redford, D. *Pharaonic King—Lists, Annals and Day Books: A Contribution to the Egyptian Sense of History* (Mississauga, Canada, 1986).

Yadin, Y. *The Art of Warfare in Biblical Lands in Light of Archaeological Study* (New York, 1963).

Chapter II—Egypt in the Ramesside Age

Alfred, C. *Jewels of the Pharaohs* (London, 1971).

Bietak, M. "Urban Archaeology and the Town Problem in Ancient Egypt," in *Egyptology and the Social Sciences,* ed. K. Weeks (Cairo, 1979), pp. 97-144.

Caminos, R. *Late-Egyptian Miscellanies* (London, 1954).

Cerný, J. *Ancient Egyptian Religion* (London, 1952).

Cerný, J. *Prices and Wages in Egypt in the Ramesside Period* (Paris, 1954).

Egypt's Golden Age: The Art of Living in the New Kingdom 1558-1085 B.C. (Boston, 1982).

Frankfort, H. *Ancient Egyptian Religion, An Interpretation* (New York, 1961).

Foster, J. *Love Songs of the New Kingdom* (New York, 1974).

van der Haagen, J. K. "Rameses' Mysterious Encounter at Dawn at the Great Temple of Abu Simbel," *The Unesco Courier* (October, 1962), pp. 10-15.

Habachi, L. *Features of the Deification of Ramesses II* (Gluckstadt, 1969).

Habachi, L. *The Obelisks of Egypt: Skyscrapers of the Past* (New York, 1977).

James, T. G. H. *Pharaoh's People: Scenes from Life in Imperial Egypt* (London, 1984).

Janssen, J. *Commodity Prices from the Ramesside Period. An Economic Study of the Village of Necropolis Workmen at Thebes* (Leiden, 1975).

Kemp, B. "Imperialism and Empire in New Kingdom Egypt (c. 1575-1087 B.C.)" in *Imperialism in the Ancient World*, eds. Garnsey and Whittaker (Cambridge, 1978), pp. 7-57.

Kitchen, K. A. "From the Brickfields of Egypt," *Tyndale Bulletin* 27 (1976), pp. 137-147.

Lesko, B. *King Tut's Wine Cellar* (Berkeley, 1977).

Lichtheim, M. *Ancient Egyptian Literature: A Book of Readings, Vols. I-III* (Berkeley, 1973-80).

Lucas, A. *Ancient Egyptian Materials and Industries* 4th ed., rev. and enlarged by J. R. Harris (London, 1962).

Montet, P. *Everyday Life in Egypt in the Days of Ramesses the Great.* 1958 (Philadelphia, 1981).

Nims, C. *Thebes of the Pharaohs* (New York, 1965).

O'Conner, D. "The Geography of Settlement in Ancient Egypt," in *Man, Settlement, and Urbanism*, eds. P. Ucko et al. (London, 1972), pp. 681-698.

Redford, D. "Studies in Relations between Palestine and Egypt during the First Millennium B.C. I. The Taxation System of Solomon," in *Studies on the Ancient Palestinian World*, eds. J. Wevers and D. Redford (Toronto, 1972), pp. 141-156.

Riefstahl, E. *Thebes in the Time of Amunhotep III* (Norman, 1964).

Romer, J. *Ancient Lives: Daily Life in Egypt of the Pharaohs* (New York, 1984).

Sauneron, S. *The Priests of Ancient Egypt* (New York, 1960).

Simpson, W. K. ed. *The Literature of Ancient Egypt* (New Haven and London, 1972).

Smith, H. S. "Society and Settlement in Ancient Egypt; in *Man, Settlement, and Urbanism* eds. P. Ucko et al. (London, 1972), pp. 705-719.

Trigger, B. G. et al. *Ancient Egypt: A Social History* (Cambridge, 1983).

Chapter III—Quest for Immortality

Andrews, C. *Egyptian Mummies* (London, 1984).

Balout, L., Robert, C. and Desroches-Noblecourt, C., et al. *La Momie de Ramses II* (Paris, 1985), includes English abstract.

Bierbrier, M. *The Tomb Builders of the Pharaohs* (London, 1982).

Cerný, J. *A Community of Workmen at Thebes in the Ramesside Period* (Cairo, 1973).

Edwards, A. *A Thousand Miles up the Nile.* 1891 (Los Angeles, 1983).

Fagan, B. *The Rape of the Nile* (New York, 1975).

Greener, L. *High Dam over Nubia* (New York, 1962).

Harris, J. E., and Weeks, K. *X-Raying the Pharaohs* (London, 1973).

MacQuitty, W. *Abu Simbel* (London, 1965).

Mekhitarian, A. *Egyptian Painting* (Geneva, 1978).

Romer, J. *Valley of the Kings* (New York, 1981).

Index

Photographers

Jon Abbott
pp. vi-vii, 21, 22-23, 24-25 bottom, 27 lower right, 30, 33, 35 middle and bottom, 37 top, 38-39, 41, 43, 47, 48 top, 50-51, 52, 54 top and bottom, 56 upper left, 57 bottom, 58, 59 top, 60, 61, 62-63, 64, 66 lower right, 67, 68-69, 70-71, 72, 73, 74, 75 top, 76 top, 77 middle left, 78 top, 79, 80, 86, 87, 89 top and bottom, 94-95, 96, 97, 98, 99, 100-101, 102 top, 107 upper left, upper right, bottom, 108, 109 bottom, 111, 112 right, 114, 119, 120-121, 123

Sharon Avery
p. 5 lower right

Glen A. Campbell
pp. 2 upper left and right, 3 upper right and bottom, 4 lower left and lower right, 5 upper left, upper right and lower left, 7, 10

William Eggleston (Memphis Brooks Museum of Art Collection)
pp. 12-13, 14-15, 16, 17, 18-19, 20

Rita E. Freed
pp. 37 bottom, 75 middle left, 88

Kenneth S. Graetz, City of Montreal
cover, pp. ii, 129, 131-133, 135-137, 139, 141-145, 147, 149-151, 153-155, 157-159, 161-189, 191-201, 203-208

Margaret Nutt Moore
pp. 2 lower left and lower right, 4 upper right

Gary Richardson
p. 90 upper left

Institutions

The British Museum
pp. 25 upper, 55, 116 top

The Brooklyn Museum
pp. 31, 56 bottom, 78 bottom, 102 bottom (photographed by David Loggie for The Brooklyn Museum Mut Expedition), 104 (photographed by David Loggie for The Brooklyn Museum Mut Expedition), 105 (photographed by David Loggie for The Brooklyn Museum Mut Expedition), 106, 112 left

Center of Documentation and Studies on Ancient Egypt (C.E.D.A.E.)
pp. 27 upper left (Neg. 16879), 40 (Neg. 12263), 42 (Neg. 10638), 48 middle (Neg. 6865), 53 top (Neg. 8567), 65 upper right (Neg. 13233), middle left (Neg. 12139), 66 upper left (Neg. 10603), 84 (Neg. 11777), 116 bottom (Neg. 16968)

Cleveland Museum of Art
p. 103 (Gift of the John Huntington Art and Polytechnic Trust)

Egypt Exploration Society—Rijksmuseum van Oudheden, Leiden Expedition to the New Kingdom Necropolis at Saqqara
p. 45

Egyptian Antiquities Organization
p. 1

Manning/Ciani-Kaiser
pp. 3 upper left, 4 upper left

Manning/Pleskow
pp. 28 upper left, upper right, bottom, 46, 90 upper right, 92, 109 top

The Metropolitan Museum of Art, New York
pp. 85, 93 (Egyptian Expedition of The Metropolitan Museum of Art Rogers Fund, 1930)

Courtesy Dr. Gamal Mokhtar, Egyptian Antiquities Organization, Cairo
p. 53 lower, 117

Musee du Louvre, Paris
pp. 56 upper right, 76 bottom, 81

Musei Vaticani
p. 26

Museo Egizio, Turin (Chomon-Perino Photograph)
pp. 24 left, 32, 59 middle, 77 bottom

Pelizaeus-Museum, Hildesheim
pp. 35 top, 57 top

Staatliche Sammlung Agyptischer Kunst, Munich
p. 82 (photo by Dietrich Wildung)

Ramesses the Great

Distributed by
St. Luke's Press
1407 Union, Suite 401
Memphis, Tennessee 38104